WHEN GREENWICH VILLAGE WAS OURS!

WHEN GREENWICH VILLAGE WAS OURS!

(Memories from Those Who Grew Up There)

ALFRED CANECCHIA

Copyright © 2022 by Alfred Canecchia.

Library of Congress Control Number:		2021924805
ISBN:	Hardcover	978-1-6698-0362-1
	Softcover	978-1-6698-0361-4
	eBook	978-1-6698-0360-7

All rights reserved. No part of this book may be reproduced or transmitted in any form or by any means, electronic or mechanical, including photocopying, recording, or by any information storage and retrieval system, without permission in writing from the copyright owner.

Any people depicted in stock imagery provided by Getty Images are models, and such images are being used for illustrative purposes only. Certain stock imagery © Getty Images.

Print information available on the last page.

Rev. date: 12/13/2021

To order additional copies of this book, contact:
Xlibris
844-714-8691
www.Xlibris.com
Orders@Xlibris.com

836084

THIS BOOK IS DEDICATED TO

Greenwich Villagers of every era.
We lived in a special environment.
We now realize, its effect on us had
no limitations, from distance and time.

Special thanks to Gary & Kate Lazarus
for well needed technical assistance.

When we fail to tell stories,
we risk forgetting who we are, where
we came from and the magic of what
we had.

Contents

Introduction xv

Peter Arcuri
Thompson Street 1

Richard (Little Rich) Artigiani
The Best Of Times 8

George (Butch) Barbezat
What A Change! 9

Sandra Briand
Air Cycling 13

Thomas Bruno
My Neighborhood 15

Alfred Canecchia
Rainbows Over Venice 19

Carole Canecchia
Fire Escape Window 35

Linda Canessa
Papa Didn't Preach! 38

Michael Carbone
Greenwich Village Vignettes-Continued 39

Lorraine Catalano
    There's No Place Like Home 42

Anthony DeCamillo
    The Crying Knish Man 46

Paula DeNicola
    Greenwich Village, My Magical Kingdom 50

Paul De Paolo
    64 MacDougal 56

Kathleen Firth
    The Starfish/Just The Friend I Needed 57

Dennis Genovese
    Father Albanese & The Little Girl 64

Dominick Joseph Genovese
    Growing Up In Greenwich Village 67

David Hunt
    Uptown Came Downtown My Time In The Village 70

Rocco John Iacovone
    Physics 101 73

Robert Leake
    Call To The Local DJ 78

Carla Lewis
    I Know How Great It Is! 81

PHOTO GALLERY

Richard Lorraine
    Growing Up In Greenwich Village 112

John Marsicovetere
    My Life In Greenwich Village 115

Charles Messina
    The Bomber Boys 127

Frederick (Freddy Bop) Nocetti
    I Wouldn't Change A Thing 135

David Noferi
    Leroy Street Pool 139

Louis Nunez
    Remembrances Of A Village Kid 143

Jean Paladino
    The Village 147

Ricardo Pecora
    Does Anybody Speak Spanish? 151

Robert Perazzo
    Holy Saturday 156

Dominick Perruccio
    The Summer Of 68 158

Francine Raggi
    Do Black People Cry Black Tears Do Bad Things
    Happen To Good People? 169

Antonia Rosa
    Being Married To Tony Orlando 172

Ralph Sabatino
    A Unique Place 174

Mitzi Schuster
    Happy Days 178

Roger Segalini
　　Growing Up In The Village In The 1950'S 180

Salvatore Tofano
　　John's Pizzeria – Two Jouneys From Different Directions ... 182

Joseph Turchiano
　　Sweet Sixteen Party November 29, 1963 192

Paul Volpe
　　Macdougal Between Bleecker & W. 3rd St.'s 194

Yolanda Volpe
　　Stuck In A Locker 196

Carol Ann Zuar
　　Mother Doesn't Always Know What's Best 198

　　Contributors 201

INTRODUCTION

by Alfred Canecchia

"When Greenwich Village Was Ours" is a collection of anecdotes, essays, short stories and remembrances from and by people who grew up or lived in the Village during the formative years of their lives. It is about a place that was a real neighborhood before gentrification, urbanization and the commercialization of New York City neighborhoods made these communities unrecognizable to those who once lived there. This is a time period before huge corporations were the only ones who could afford the exorbitant rents of today. It was when Mom and Pop enterprises dominated the landscape. A time when we contributing writers had pride in our neighborhood, which was highly self-sufficient and safe, and above all absolutely unique. Italian food, bread, pastry and pizza shops flourished. Clubs to see comedians, musicians and theatres for drama abounded. Street artists as well as sculptors and minstrels were omnipresent. In the flux of time all things change. Especially in a cosmopolitan city that has always welcomed immigrants the world over. "Give me your tired, your poor, your huddled masses yearning to breathe free."* Greenwich Village is one of the many neighborhoods that lived up to this ideal.

These are true stories that happened in Greenwich Village when it was ours. And because of these memories, we know as long as it remains in our hearts, that it will always belong to those who lived and grew up there.

- *Emma Lazarus, "The New Colossus."

Peter Arcuri

Thompson Street

I can vividly recall one warm summer afternoon as I stood eating a hot dog on the corner of Thompson Street and Washington Square South. It was 1970. As I enjoyed my hot dog, I was instructed to eat only half and return with the uneaten portion to give to a guy in a van parked around the corner. When I returned with the uneaten portion, the guy in the van was outraged! He drove the van to the hot dog stand and began to curse, "You _____ sucker, you're not buying my onions!"

I was instructed to tip over his hot dog cart, so I obeyed with great enthusiasm. I'll always remember the boiling water pouring on the street, buns and dogs rolling everywhere. The guy in the van was GI Joe Sternfeld, a Jewish mobster who spoke out of the side of his mouth. With GI Joe, every other word was a curse. He was also Tommy "Ryan" Eboli's driver.

When I was 16, Thompson Street was the center of my life. Eboli was the head of the Genovese crime family. Thompson Street was, and remains, only eight blocks long, bordered by Washington Square South and 4th Street on the North and Canal Street as its southern border. However, Thompson Street snaked its way through four different neighborhoods. NYU from Washington Square South to 3rd Street owned everything except the Judson Memorial Hall where we played basketball, went to the dentist and received our vaccinations. Third Street to West Houston, crossing Bleecker, was the heart of

Greenwich Village, home to the beatniks, hippies and preppies. Crossing West Houston brought you into the South Village, now known as SoHo. South of Houston, past Prince to Spring Street was its own neighborhood. The North Thompson Street kids went to Our Lady of Pompeii School. South Thompson kids went to St. Anthony of Padua School, and the most southern kids went to St. Alphonse's on lower Thompson and Canal Street.

I lived on the cusp of Thompson and West Houston, so I went to St. Anthony's. My classmates were mostly Italian. Some were Irish, and in the late 50's we saw an influx of Puerto Ricans, Mexicans, Portuguese and Cubans. Our melting pot was most unique. Sunday's aromas of meatballs, macaroni, rice, beans and fried bananas would waft through the buildings. We all got along. One of my best friends to this day is a Cuban kid who arrived in 1959. Our gang was like a United Nations Conference – every ethnic group was represented.

My parents moved to Thompson Street after WW2, when apartments were scarce. Their first apartment was only considered to be temporary, but lasted twenty years. My family history on Thompson Street dates back to the early 1900's. My uncle and his brothers, fresh from Sicily, opened La Nova Grocery on 100 Thompson Street. My dad was born on King Street and worked there as a kid. In the 1960's they moved the store to 555 2nd Avenue, and it was renamed Todaro Bros. I was lucky to own a bike and luckier still to park it at Jean's Pocketbook Store across the street from me. For a couple of dollars a month, she would store the neighborhood's bikes and strollers. Everyone had a key. As I recall it now, I wonder, how would that work today?

The store closed when it became infested with mice. I used to pedal north from my house toward Bleecker Street. I knew every crack, bump and groove in the concrete. There was even a horse stable a few buildings north of mine. The horses would crap up and down Thompson Street. The smell of horse droppings would lure the rats out of the building, so I would always cross the street to avoid them. The opposition to rats runs deep in every New Yorker's veins. We had many derelict hotels. The ones on my corner were the famous Mills Hotel and the Bleecker Hotel. We had a chicken market that added to the smell of urine and couldn't quite disguise the overarching aroma of spent, cheap liquor bottles and horse feces. I'd hang a right on Bleecker and spy The Bitter End, The Other End, The Mori Building, The Bleecker Street Cinema, and many, many cafes as I rode my bike. The original entrance to The Village Gate was on Thompson, just opposite the stable that housed the horses. Just north on Bleecker was The Back Fence and the slaughterhouse for the chickens. You could buy anything live, have it slaughtered, quartered, drained, butchered and ready for that evening's meal.

Oh the scents of Thompson Street! My bike rides would continue right onto La Guardia Place, in essence, West Broadway. This was long before Morton Williams was there. Back then, it was Grand Union and then NYU took over. There were razed buildings across on LaGuardia, now 505 LaGuardia Place that housed an old army and navy surplus store. As kids, we would play in the debris and build underground forts. Our Imaginations ran wild with each new bit of dirt we would unearth.

Riding at full speed, I would turn right again on West Houston. On the corner was Lillian Hardware, the exact spot where this old man would sit outside most days. One day in 1961, I stopped and talked to him. He said he was over 100 years old and that he had been in the Civil war. I was 7 and was very impressed. Much later, I would calculate that he would have been a child fighting in the war in 1861. I was still impressed!

Arturo's Pizza was located on MacDougal and West Houston during the late 1960's prior to its present location. In its place was home to Hi's Bicycle Shop. Most of the Thompson Street area was still very Italian, save for the sprinklings of other ethnicities. This was long before supermarkets, so we shopped in mom and pop specialty stores. Ralph's Baccala Store, Frank's Butcher, Molinari's Grocery Store. There were pork stores and bakeries everywhere, each contributing to the acrid but comforting aromas that made Thompson Street home. Next to Rocco's Restaurant, Alfonse's Candy Store would briefly close on Sunday afternoon to allow the family to enjoy their Sunday dinner.

One of my earliest memories is of Vito Genovese sitting outside my building, operating the attached store where he sold bootleg cigarettes and conducted street business. My building was one of the taller ones, on the block, so suicides and murders were common. When a person jumped, fell, or was pushed, they would tumble a ways then get tangled in the clotheslines strewn across the courtyard. I remember a woman who jumped or got pushed and predictably got tangled in the mess of lines. The police removed the body but left her slipper behind. I remember rushing home from school each day to see if the slipper was still there. It remained for over a year in the courtyard.

The Mafia was everywhere on Thompson Street, which made it an extremely safe neighborhood. In addition to the Boys, everyone watched out for each other. I had 30 mothers growing up. Long before "safe" houses, we had Social Clubs. Actual chartered venues selling booze, playing card games and organized dancing. The Venus Club was on Thompson Street, just south of Bleecker. The Sky Top Club was there too, but south of Houston, across the street from Frankie & Louie's club. South of Prince was the 400 Club. All except the Venus Club were operated by neighborhood guys. The Venus Club belonged to Vincent "the Chin" Gigante. As a kid, along with the entire neighborhood, I vowed to never refer to him by that name.

I made a mistake a year later when referring to him by rubbing my chin to gain entrance to the Copacabana to see the Four Seasons. Of course, they sat us right up front, and Frankie Valli came by to shake my hand. I caught a harsh slap in the face the next day when I was called to his club at 208 Sullivan Street. As his heavy hand left my face, he said, "How's your mom? Send my love." Ironically, I was not related to him but was with his cousin and 14 year old niece while trying to access the Copa.

Another story I remember took place at a Fourth of July party on my roof at 172 Thompson Street. Our apartment was on the top floor, just one short staircase to the roof. My dad was a chef and would make pizzas from scratch and deliver them to the roof. Vinnie always supplied the fireworks. We used to throw them off the roof often without looking. When we were about 10 years old, Vinnie's oldest son's pants caught on fire. Apparently, he had fireworks in his pocket! Vinnie came running over and started tearing his son's pockets off. He was Vinnie and he was the hero of the neighborhood. His four sisters-in-law were scattered along my block on Thompson Street, so I was like an adopted nephew. We all knew he was the head of the Five Families – it took the FBI 30 years to figure it out. He was not feared like John Gotti but loved and respected by all. During the Venus Club's years of operation, Eddie "The Blonde" took over running the club. I actually worked for him for a time. I ran the club in the early hours up till midnight, then we would clear out. Every time I would ask Eddie a question he would respond, "Use your own discretion." I was 16 at the time, and all the kids would drink, play cards, play the jukebox, and make out. I didn't play cards or drink, so I was perfect for the job. I collected 10 percent of every pot for the house. I also ran the Sky Top Club and collected the same amount from Ned. The Sky Top Club was run by Nunzio "Ned" Genovese, my future neighbor on Broome Street. He also ran Milady's Bar. Whenever I hung out to play pool at Milady's, Ned would always make fashion suggestions – match this color and cut your hair! Ned was watching out for me. He turned into my landlord and lived across the hall from me when my family moved to 552 Broome Street. This little stretch of Thompson near Prince was run by the Eastside Boys. I never knew why.

A later Fourth of July, we were hanging outside Milady's when someone lit a case of firecrackers. Well, they thought it was a case. But, unfortunately, it was a case of M80's. Every window within 100 feet of the explosion was broken, except for the windows of Milady's. Talk about neighborhood protection!

In 1966, when I was 12, my family moved to Broome Street, between 6th Avenue and Varick Street. I was forced to desert my beloved Thompson Street. I became a Broome Street Bomber. Luckily, just a short hop past 6th Avenue was Lower Thompson, a different culture, more street and gutsier. I had been a northern Thompson Street boy my entire life and attended the Morosini Club on Sullivan – kindergarten, after school basketball. We were

1969 Kiwanis Basketball Champs for the Morosini Club. Lower Thompson had less mom and pop stores but more neighborhood car buffs and bikers. It had an edge to it. It was dark and deserted on Lower Thompson. The neighborhood guys and bikers would gather outside the laundromat at 57 Thompson and drink and guard the lower end of the street all the way to Canal Street.

1967 was the summer of love and I was living on Broome. Thompson and Bleecker were experiencing anti-war protests. Almost every day, Washington Square Park was buzzing with activists. Thompson south of Houston was business as usual, still clinging to Doo-Wop music, which could often be heard outside of the clubs at night. You could walk a block and stumble upon bands of boys harmonizing in any little alley for better acoustics.

The other Band of Boys had their various businesses in the street. Numbers was the big one. You would bet the last three numbers of the Total Mutual Handling at any given racetrack. Then, as the numbers came out around 2-3 o'clock when the racetracks closed, runners would run with their fingers in the air announcing which number came out. It was hilarious! On occasion, I was given a paper bag to bring to a certain club. I never questioned anything or knew what was going on. It always felt like the safest place on earth.

I was given the name "The Kid" because I was young and hanging out with the big boys. Mikey Urgo, who ran the Chateau Club on Sullivan Street, called me that when he hired me at 13 to run his record store on Spring Street just off Thompson. I still refer to him as "Boss". The sign outside read International Discount Sales. It was not! The back room was for gaming slips on sports bets, loan sharking and various other things. Vinnie would have his Saturday haircut at Rocky's Barber on Spring Street. Not everyone knew that Saturday afternoon on Spring Street was heavily guarded.

My dad got really sick in 1967 and died two years later in 1969. He was the food and beverage director of the newly opened New York Hilton. His secretary, Nancy, loved the banquet rooms and decided to have her wedding there. Her brother was Tommy "Ryan" Eboli, who was at the time, the head of the Genovese Family. My dad attended the wedding, and everything went well, thank God! Tommy used to hang out in a café on Thompson, Angela's Café, just south of Bleecker, across from the Venus Club. In July, Angela, who was Italian by birth, would travel to Italy wearing a fur coat in the heat of summer! Inside the liner of her fur coat was cash. She was the mule that moved Tommy's cash to Italy. Her husband Charlie suspected she was having an affair with Tommy. Charlie got drunk one night and was so filled with jealous rage he wanted to kill Tommy. I was at the jukebox, trying to ignore the conversation, when Frankie "Bots" another of Vinnie's henchmen, handed him a gun to complete the task. Tommy's days were numbered – but Charlie backed down.

One day I was brazen enough to approach him and introduce myself. As I said my name. Peter Arcuri, same as my dad, his eyes lit up and then asked how my dad was doing? I told him that he died. I was now under his wing, so to speak. We would have espresso together. He taught me gin rummy and how to "speculate" when playing cards. He took me to Frank's Barber on Thompson for a proper haircut. In fact, if your hair was too long, one of the Boys would gladly give you a trim. His fingers were manicured and painted with clear nail polish. He wore beautiful Italian suits and straw hats. He first hired me to work for Tryan vending machines. All the clubs and bars had jukeboxes that he owned. I would collect the money, do minor repairs, and change the selections of the 45 records. He introduced me to GI Joe Sternfeld, his driver. GI Joe ran the hot dog stands around the city. Tommy Ryan met his fate one night in 1972 in Crown heights, Brooklyn. He was shot and killed, and the only witness was his driver, GI Joe Sternfeld. Another face would soon appear on Thompson Street.

Richard (Little Rich) Artigiani

The Best Of Times

Thinking about the past
Remembering the good old days
The good nuns of Pompeii
Father Cogo and the Friday night dances
With my partner, Linda.
Lunch at the Morisini Club
Pizza from Polichetti's on Carmine Street
Hot cooked salami sandwiches
At Bosco's on Bleecker
Pastry and Italian ices at Rocco's
Then it was off to Cardinal Hayes H.S.
In the Bronx with my buddies
Al (Butchie) Canecchia, Donald Benedetto
And Gerard Madison
These are some of the lasting memories
I have of being raised in a great neighborhood.
Those were the best of times!

George (Butch) Barbezat

What A Change!

It was August 1955, a hot and humid day, and I was happy because it was my ninth birthday. My mother, my aunt and my three cousins, who lived across the hall, were preparing my birthday party. My aunt was the oldest sister in a family of nine siblings, my mother being the youngest. The cousins were all in their late teens. We all lived at 165 W 4th Street. It was a nice building and all five kids coming to the party lived there. The party started at 3 pm and ended at six. The one thing missing was my father. We waited until ten that night when he finally arrived home. He was drunk, as usual, and my parents started to argue. Little did I know that this would be a monumental change in my life. The argument ended. My mother packed some clothes in a paper bag and we were off to my grandmother's apartment. It was three short blocks away across 6th Avenue, the dividing line. The change had started and it would prove to be a drastic one.

West 4th Street was a busy pedestrian street connecting Seventh and Sixth Avenues. There weren't many kids to play with at my grandmother's. Most of my playmates lived at my former address. My grandmother's apartment at 122 MacDougal was across from Minetta Lane between Third and Bleecker Streets. This block was filled with tenements and store fronts. It was a little town of its own. It had three restaurants, four bars, many coffee houses, a bakery, a social club, two candy stores, a liquor store, vegetable store and pizzeria. We wanted for nothing. The noise and clamor of the city was ever present. People fighting in the street, others playing guitars or singing and still others reciting poetry. The occasional motor cycle gang came rampaging through and there was always an overabundance of tourists. The difference between W 4th Street and MacDougal was like night and day. This was just the beginning.

The apartment we abandoned on 4th Street was comparably modern. It had a bathroom with a tub and shower, steam heat, a refrigerator and one of the first air conditioners. Although, it would only work for a short while before it blew the circuit and the entire building would lose power. On MacDougal Street we kept our food cold in an old fashioned ice box. My job was to change the melting water once a day and replenish the ice every couple of days. We had no steam heat. Instead, there was a beautiful pot belly stove, in one room that used wood or coal, when we could afford to buy such items. The stove was capable of heating only two of the four rooms. A bath was a luxury accessible maybe once a week since it was in the kitchen. In an Italian family, someone is always in the kitchen. I took a sponge bath every night on a piece of newspaper. Last, but not least, we had to share the hallway toilet with the apartment across the hall. Thank goodness they were relatives: aunt, uncle and cousins. All in all, these new obstacles, just made this nine year old a lot tougher.

The apartment overlooked the playground on MacDougal and Minetta Lane. The Lane was the place to play for all the kids and there must have been over a hundred. We played everything on this dirty street that was once a stream. The change from playing board games and hit the penny with a rubber ball on 4th Street to the range of activities I now was engaged in was revolutionary. Here we played stickball, stoop ball, punch ball, slap ball, relay races, hop scotch, jump rope, tag, buck-buck, football and roller skating. I built scooters out of milk crates with a whole bunch of new kids.

The first kids I met lived in the tenement next to mine. They were: Richard Benedetti, Bill Genovese, Joe Piazza and Mike Russo. Bill Genovese and Richie Benedetti would remain my friends through High School. They introduced me to all the kids on the Lane and were my protectors. We played from morning until night. Taking breaks only for lunch and dinner. In the morning we would choose teams. These teams stayed together for the day, unless someone had to go shopping for their mother or baby sit. We tried to play football in the fall and winter, and some other form of ball during the spring and summer. Stoop ball was our favorite. We played on different stoops with different rules. Also, in the spring, we would roller skate and build scooters.

For me, these changes were drastic. I went from playing in the hallway to being a street kid. We would eat lunch on a stoop or curb. While playing, we sometimes fell into dirty water or animal feces that was on the street. We got up, wiped ourselves off, and continued to play. Each day was an adventure because you never knew which kids would come to play or what games we would engage in.

A social change for me was in trying to become friends with so many different kids. Some were very easy to get along with while others were shy and reluctant. A few were tough bullies who just wanted to beat you up. Emotionally, it took a toll on me. I just wanted to get along with everybody. So I found a release in a physical nature. I was becoming a good athlete. The more I played the better I played and the more friends I made. They would pick me for their teams and I would pick them for mine. Even the girls would pick me for hop scotch or jump rope because I had stamina and could last long.

Psychologically, I was maturing much faster on MacDougal Street, because of all the adjustments I had to make. Plus, there was so much happening on the street besides the games. Just by listening and observing I learned a lot. These streets were a gold mine of knowledge.

There were things I heard and saw for the first time. Men and women fighting in the street with blood flowing like water. The noise of motor cycle gangs, sometimes fifty or more in number, sounded like rolling thunder. Junkies shooting up on Minetta Lane and more than one dead body left on the street in the wake of rampant neighborhood drug use. Rich people pulling up in roadsters or Rolls Royces to go into Minetta Tavern, Café Reggio, or the many coffee houses that dotted the landscape. I saw movie stars like Elizabeth Taylor and Kirk Douglas from time to time. There were all sorts of "beatniks" drinking coffee while sitting for hours in conversation or listening to poetry being recited. Tourists, heading for the Café Wha?, curiously eyed us little "rag-a-muffins", playing on the street.

There were people interrupting our games who made musical history One day, a skinny guy all dressed in black with black boots, walked right through our play area. Later, I found out, he was the poet and songwriter, Bob Dylan. Another time we were playing slap ball when a tall black man carrying a guitar and a jug of wine sat down to watch. He began to hum and play, sing and drink. One day while watching a concert on TV I recognized the same man. It was Richie Havens.

We were choosing teams one day for stick-ball when three people stopped to talk right where we were setting up to play. They were two men and a woman with blonde hair. We had seen them before stopping under a lamppost or in an alcove. They lingered for a while harmonizing and scribbling in a notebook. When we were in High School, a friend from MacDougal Street, told me they were a famous trio called Peter, Paul & Mary.

The social, emotional, physical, psychological changes from my ninth birthday to entering High School were monumental. I went from a non-athletic, shy, fearful child to a self-confident athlete with good person to person skills. I also credit the time I spent during winters at the Morosini Children's Aid Center as formative. Helping me to "never work a day in my life" because I ended up doing something that I loved. I became a Physical Education Teacher and coached college basketball for over fifty years.

• • • • • • • ● ○ ○ ○ ○ ○ ○ ○ ○ ○

Sandra Briand

Air Cycling

One really hot summer day my girlfriend, Louise, and I were walking through Washington Square Park hunting for the Good Humor ice cream cart. We loved their Creamsicles. I guess we were about 13 or 14 years old, at the time, which would place the year at 1958 or 59. In that time frame the style of the day was to wear toreador pants (Spandex by today's standard.) I remember I was wearing red skin tight pants and a black sleeveless blouse. Out of nowhere, what seemed to be a huge Black man, picked me up by the waist and said, "You're the most adorable thing I've seen all day." My legs were running but I was still being held up in the air, while Louise was crying and screaming. "Please put her down!"

Washing Johnny's Car

I grew up on Thompson Street, between Bleecker and Houston Streets. The Village Gate on one corner and The Bitter End around the other. When I was a teenager, I was 1/5th of a group of girlfriends: Gerry, Louise, Helen, Irene and me. We spent most of our waking hours together and often slept over each other's apartments. We dressed in the same manner, wearing similar clothes and hair styles. The fashion of the day was very long hair worn in double pony tails (one underneath the other) that hung long and low down our backs.

Every day after school, and every weekend, we could all be found at a pizza store on Carmine Street (Village Pizza) where the owner, Dominick, would let us spend hours sitting in a back booth, playing the Jukebox while nursing our Cherry Cokes. I'm sure every once in a while we actually bought some slices of pizza.

During those years my grammar school boyfriend was "Danny Mouse" (who some years later I would marry and have three daughters with.) Danny was the younger brother of the neighborhood heart throb "Johnny," who worked around the corner at Luke's Garage on Seventh Avenue South. He was also part of a singing group known as the Young Tones and drove a white Ford convertible which was usually parked at Luke's. He was looked up to by the neighborhood girls as a local celebrity. My friends and I would saunter over to the garage/gas station, and beg him to take us for a ride in his car with the top down. We wanted to be seen by as many of our peers as was possible. Johnny always stipulated that if we wanted a ride, we would have to wash his car first. We were always happy to do so if it meant getting a spin in the roadster.

That scenario played out many times and true to his word after the car was spanking clean he would take us cruising through the neighborhood or up the old elevated West Side Highway. Oh! We were so cool! I don't know how long the rides lasted, but I think I'd be safe in saying they were too short for us, and too long for Johnny.

· · · · · · · ● ○ ○ ○ ○ ○ ○ ○ ○ ○

Thomas Bruno

My Neighborhood

I wrote this song several years ago. It tells the story of growing up and moving on in Greenwich Village NY, through the 1950's, 60's and 70's.

I am writing a biographical explanation for each verse of the song. "Given No Choice."

1st Verse

> Thank you Father for slapping me
> While I prayed on bended knee
> If that's the way you save souls
> Shows why you're shrinking rolls

Growing up under the Roman Catholic Church in Greenwich Village, you were expected to have your first Holy Communion and confirmation.

During the ritual of confirmation the bishop slaps your face to remind you of your vows and commitment to the church.

One day, my mother kept me home from school to help her clean the alleyway between our apartments. This had to be done every week because the feral cats would make a mess out there. This created an unsanitary condition. When I finished I went bowling with my friends. A bowling ball accidentally fell on my finger crushing it. My mother took me to the local doctor who put my hand in a cast and sling. The next day Sister Hilda Marie, my fourth grade teacher, told me that God punished for skipping school by crushing my finger. She then made me take a penmanship test. The passing grade was a 70 and she gave me a 69. In my heart this is why, I believe, the Catholic Church is losing members. God would not want a child punished and humiliated if he represents love and kindness.

2nd Verse

> Just a squire from New York City
> Serving Rock and Rolls Royalty
> Helping to find inspired spirits
> To move on from broken dreams

Greenwich Village was changing. I had the pleasure of meeting and knowing Richie Havens. Around 1970 he took over the lease at the Café Wha? His road manager Dennis Persich brought me in to help Nancy Havens in the club. They taught me how to do sound and lights. This opportunity opened up a whole new world to a kid from the neighborhood. I went on to do sound and lights for The Other End and to tour with many bands as a road manager and sound engineer. These include: Carly Simon, The Band, The Pschedelic Furs, Minh Deville, Jack Bruce and many others.

Chorus

> He wanted to be Robert L. Coco
> A slap turned him into a little itch
> From a life of hope and happiness
> He ended up in a shallow ditch

I had always looked up to my oldest cousin. He was a shining light to me. He was friendly, personable and a gifted artist. During an incident in school, the priest slapped him cuffing his ear, this caused him to lose hearing in that ear. Afterwards all the adults defended the priest believing him to be a representative of God. My cousin was never the same. Whenever he would find himself in jeopardy he used the alias Robert L. Coco. After the aforementioned incident, he started using drugs. Eventually, because of methadone, bone cancer took his life.

3rd Verse

> Given back some family traditions
> A road of music inspired nights
> Lights of the world's big cities
> And Dylan's I Shall Be Free

Richie Havens not only introduced me to the world of music. He also introduced me to Grand Master Ronald M. Taganashi, founder of American Te, Goju Ryu Karate Heaven and Earth Society.

Master Taganashi usually only accepted students who were brought into the school by his Black Belts. Because of his respect for Richie, Master Taganashi met me in Central Park and after several hours of conversation agreed to let me train. I began training in 1973 and no matter how long I was away touring the world I was always welcomed back into the Dojo. Master Taganashi's Dojo traditions allowed us all to become a family. The combination of music, travel and training took me past the traumas of my youth and the constraints of the neighborhood, allowing me to become my true self. As expressed in Dylan's "I Shall Be Free." This song still resonates today.

4th Verse

> Back to the squire from the city
> Bright lights, Rock and Roll Nights
> He didn't confuse fame for religion
> But found his soul under bright stage lights

Exposure to the bright lights of Rock and Roll could have taken me down the wrong path. Yet through my martial arts training and the good people who've entered my life, I have been able to achieve security, contentment and gratitude.

The song "Given No Choice" is copy written

Words and Music, Thomas L. Bruno. Additional musical assistance from Edward Colaci.

• • • • • • • • ● ○○○○○○ ○ ○ ○

Alfred Canecchia

Rainbows Over Venice

It was the summer of 1955. The heat was melting the tar on the roof of 15 Jones Street where my mother and sister were lying, basking in the sun. The transistor radio was playing the Moonglow's recording of "Sincerely." I had an appreciation for the Doo-Wop harmony style of vocalizing. Yet my attention was distracted. I was drawn to the pigeon coop that occupied a section of the roof. Men in the building kept them as a hobby. One that was slowly fading. Like many of the cultural activities that were prevalent before the Second World War, this interest would soon be a memory. Those who were born after the war were lucky. We would look back and consider this time period to be the height of our civilization. A 13,000 year period where our species, Homo sapiens, had not only dominated, but flourished. Life being as it is changes, sometimes with little warning, and other times with ominous signs. With the disastrous effects of climate change looming, this dominance would be severely challenged if not gone, just like the birds I watch fly off into the sky.

I was ten years old. I knew nothing of the world and its rhythms. Stoop Ball was all that concerned me. On Jones Street where I lived this game took prominence over all others. We played it with a fervor. The curb in front of the Greenwich Pottery House at 16 Jones provided the edifice to hit the Spaulding ball off. All the boys on the block joined in. Girls, were not part of this activity, and basically not part of our world, yet. That would come later and for some with devastating impact. For now, our universe revolved around these street games. We learned the basics from each other and the older boys (Artie Beretta, Carmine Lombardo, and Ronnie (Pepper) Torre) who still participated. Soon they would move on like their peers had done. Off to High School, work, family obligations and involvement with the opposite sex. For now, such responsibilities were worlds away, as far as I was concerned.

    I liked to harmonize and enjoyed doing so with other kids who sang. We pursued this passion on street corners but also sought out hallways that produced a fine echo. Subway stations were also excellent venues. This pastime offered something creative to engage in. It kept us out of trouble and alleviated the boredom of school, homework and everyday pedestrian life. Young celebrities like Elvis were taking the culture by storm. Chuck Berry, Little Richard and other pioneers were laying the foundations of rock and roll that would explode in the next decade. Frankie Lyman & the Teenagers would hit the charts in 1956, along with the Platters and soon followed by the Drifters and the Miracles, whose lead singer, Smokey Robinson, would be a big factor in the success of Detroit's Motown Records in the 1960's. We listened to all this music on the radio and purchased 45 rpm discs to play at home. Group harmony and Doo-Wop singing was for my generation what Big Band music and dancing had been to the previous one.

    Drugs had infiltrated the neighborhood. After the war they found their way into the major urban centers. Soon the suburbs would succumb to their additive allure. The Korean skirmish brought the second wave of American GI's to be introduced to hard drugs. In the early 1960's, teenagers in Greenwich Village started experimenting with *marijuana*. It had many names: Maryjane, pot, weed, grass, smoke, dope. When I was 16, in 1961, a pound of grass cost $50. There were about 25 joints or J's in a nickel ($5) bag. The high was mystical, funny, irreverent and whimsical. It was a happy up. You felt good and got the munchies at the same time. After smoking a joint we would run through the local super market giggling and yelling, "Where the hell are the Mallomars?" There appeared to be no dangerous side effects and no cravings for something more powerful. It was basically harmless, and fit in with the cultural, artistic and bohemian ambiance of the Village. The beat poets, Ferlinghetti and Ginsberg, along with the jazz musicians had long ago found marijuana's magic and were already hip to its effects. In 1965, while touring England, Bob Dylan would turn on the Beatles to its potency. I guess we were ahead of the curve in that respect.

As we matured, the opposite sex came into view. Most of the boys had little or no experience or aptitude with affairs of the heart. This was especially true if you did not have older brothers to teach you the ropes. It was new territory in which many hearts and feelings would be given a rough and tumble ride. Some lives were shattered from unrequited love or star crossed matches. Some people abused themselves with drugs and or alcohol after coming out on the short end of a love affair. My H.S. buddy De Leon fell into this category. I asked my neighborhood girlfriend to bring a girlfriend of hers along to his 18th birthday party in 1962. We introduced him to her. He fell hard and when they broke up he began to drink heavily. It was the beginning of a lifetime of alcohol abuse. Those who had artistic outlets: music, art, writing, used those vehicles to ameliorate their loss. It gave the heartbreak a constructive expression. The lost object of one's affections, became the Muse to inspire creative rather than destructive behavior. The energy of the libido was given an alternative. I was fortunate to have those outlets and the Muse to inspire them. Unfortunately, the girl that captured my heart did not seem to have the time for me, or the passion and desire to pursue whatever feelings she may have harbored. I would seek comfort elsewhere and eventually find my solace in the arts.

When I was about 15-years old, singing in a group, harmonizing and putting a band together was my major artistic endeavor. When I reflect back on those times I remember my friend Danny. I first met him when I was 16 and he was 17. I had been singing background harmony with my cousin Dennis Genovese and another local musical talent, Ralph Sabatino. We were being coached by Robert Andriani.

He was two years my senior. A gifted singer with a sweet tenor voice who also was adept on the guitar and played piano. Ralph was also a good piano player while Dennis and I were just getting interested in playing the guitar. Robert Andriani, Ziggy, as he was known in the neighborhood was singing with John Marsicovetere, formerly lead singer of the Young Tones, and now with a regrouping of those lads with Ziggy singing tenor. He had replaced the original tenor, Gilbert Rivera, who was now second tenor. Rounding out the quartet was Luis Lugo, the original bass singer of the Young Tones. They would be renamed Marci & the Mates and would record for Big Top Records in 1962, with songs written by the famous duo of Doc Pomus and Mort Schuman. But that was yet to come. For the moment, we were learning harmonies in the hallway of Downing Street Park, off of Carmine Street. It was in the fall months of 1960 and I was 15 years old. We loved what we were doing and anything seemed possible. There was a fine echo in that hallway and Ziggy would give us our singing parts from the chords he played on his Harmony guitar. There was also a standup piano in a room on the second floor that he and Ralph would sometimes play.

We learned the background vocals to popular songs and oldies which are now considered Doo-Wop classics. "The Ten Commandments of Love," "Blueberry Sweet" and "Down on My Knees" were part of our repertoire. Ziggy was honing his arranging skills which he would later craft into art with the songs he would write for Hill & Range Publishing, when he would later become apprenticed under and writing partner with the great songwriter Doc Pomus. Doc, already a legend, had written lyrics to such memorable songs as "Suspicion," "This Magic Moment" and "Save the Last Dance for Me." The demos of the songs Ziggy would write: "The Letter I Never Wrote," "Don't Tell Gabrielle," "My Heart Keeps Following You" and "King Lonely the Blue," where he not only sings lead and back ground vocals, but also plays all instruments including lead and rhythm guitars, drums, piano, bass guitar and melodica, are a testament to his ability and talent. Sometimes he would play a stand-up bass or any other instrument that happened to be lying around or left behind in the recording studio. A close listen to these recordings reveal that they are comparable to the early recordings, 1962-64, of the Beatles. The quality, musicianship and arrangements were on an equal level. That of course would all change after the Fab Four's encounter with Bob Dylan in London, in 1965. The albums that followed, "Rubber Soul" and "Revolver" would set the Beatles on a journey that would forever change not only Rock & Roll but the entire music industry. Session musicians, those who played instruments in the recording studios on pop songs composed by writing teams from the Brill Building that dominated the charts from the late 1950's till the arrival of the Beatles, and what followed them, in what was called the British Invasion, were suddenly no longer in demand. Bands were now composing and playing their own material leaving little work for these accomplished side men.

Ziggy's art was and always would be in mastering simplicity, which is an art in itself. When not working on his own original material, he would be arranging harmony and counterpoint with his understudies. Dennis was a particularly good student who would later go on to arrange, produce and record his own material and songs written with and by his musical collaborator, Karen Mantero. That partnership would begin in the mid 1970's and flourish in the 1980's. Ziggy knew our group was ready for and in need of a lead singer. He suggested someone he had casually sung with during down time from his commitment to the Young Tones. John Marsi had a younger brother Danny who also sang and had a sweet tenor voice. I remember hearing him harmonizing with Ziggy and a kid named Richie Clark in a tenement hallway. It was like listening to three angels sing!

So it came to pass that in the spring of 1961, Daniel Marsicovetere, known as "Danny Mouse," joined our group as lead singer and we labeled ourselves Danny & the Sinceres. We needed a bass singer to fill out the harmony style that was in current vogue. A classmate of mine from Our Lady of Pompeii and Cardinal Hayes H.S. filled the void. His name was Gerard Madison. Gerard was an adept rhythm guitar and ukulele player. This group would last several years. Danny was a particularly gifted Doo-Wop tenor lead with a multiple octave falsetto. He covered all the hits of Pearl McKinnon and the Kodaks, Frankie Lymon & the Teenagers and Herbie Cox & the Cleftones. His best cover was a rendition of the ballad "Gloria," recorded by Earl Carrol and the Cadillacs, Earl Lewis & the Channels and sung by every street corner harmony group that ever existed. Danny & the Sinceres cut their first demo in a recording studio on 42nd Street. The recording session cost us $50. The A side was an original composition by Ralph Sabatino titled, "Can You Spare a Kiss for a Stranger." The B side was a cover of Frankie Lyman & the Teenager's "Out in the Cold Again."

Danny was also a gritty blues singer, and later with the group the Roman Numerals, a fine bass player. But before that group formed and after the Sinceres broke up, he, along with Dennis Genovese and Al Canecchia were in a folk group called the Marsi Trio. The Marsi Trio disbanded in 1963 and Dennis, Danny, Ralph and John Hanrahan recorded a song titled "Angela" for producer Artie Ripp. The recording failed to make any noise but was a good learning experience. Artie Ripp would later go on to great success and fortune producing Billy Joel in the 1970's. In February 1964, Al Canecchia, Dennis Genovese and Danny Marsi joined up with Danny's older brother John, to form the Roman Numerals. This group was together five years and accomplished a lot in that time period. They recorded "Matchstick in a Whirlpool" and three other John Marsi compositions for Columbia Records in 1967, appeared at Carnegie Hall in 1968 with the Rock & Roll Singing Orchestral Circus, promoted by Jerry Kasenetz and Jeff Katz, the founders of Buddha Records and performed at Trudy Heller's, The Purple Onion and The Bitter End. The group was scheduled to appear on the Ed Sullivan Show but the broadcast was canceled due to the tragic assassination of Bobby Kennedy.

Danny was a great happy go lucky kind of guy. He married young at 17, in 1961, and by the end of the decade had three daughters with his first wife Sandy. The marriage broke up around 1970. The pressure of marrying young, having three children to provide for, along with the demands of work, singing and performing, took their toll. In the early 1970's Danny met his second wife, a Welch girl, who had a distinctive way of speaking the Kings English. Her real name was Joan but she called herself Pat. It always reminded me of the Beatles song, "Rocky Racoon": "her name was Magill and she called herself Lil, but everyone knew her as Nancy." I was expecting that third name to surface but it never did. Danny married Pat and *voila*, he had three more girls. Apparently males were not in his gene pool? Now he had six girls to support. He was always working but his love for music kept him involved. He fronted a band that played at weddings, bar mitzvahs anniversaries et cetera. He had left his job at Panasonic and was doing Formica work, installing kitchens, bathrooms and such. We lost touch for several years after he moved to Staten Island.

IN 1989, Danny was diagnosed with Scleroderma, a disease of the connective tissues of the body's organs. It is theorized that the toxic fumes emanating from the adhesive glue used in Formica work, enters the skin and causes this degenerative malady. The doctors who treated him said he could extend his life by moving to a warmer climate, but still they predicted he would live only ten more years. He was 45 years old at the time. His family moved to Venice Florida that year and bought a house. He continued to install kitchens and do the work he was trained to do, but now as his own boss. Dennis Genovese had moved to Northport and they were about twenty minutes away from each other. Because of this proximity, my wife Roberta and I would spend our Easter school vacations in Florida. First, visiting her parents on the East coast in Margate, then driving to the West coast to spend a day or two with Dennis and celebrate Easter Sunday on Venice Beach with the Marsi family. They always had a big group and would invite all the people who were alone to join them. There were two older women who had no other family. We affectionately called them the Pigeon Sisters. They always participated. We would bring out the guitars and play and sing at these gatherings. Whenever any of the Marsi clan assembled, music was involved. This was also the case when we would drive in the summer to visit John Marsi and his family in the Lake George area of N. Y. State. We always enjoyed going to Florida. We flew back on a plane looking forward to next year's gathering.

As time passed, Danny's condition deteriorated. His breathing suffered and he could no longer hold his breath to sing in the recording studio. As the disease advanced he was first on an oxygen tank followed by being in a wheelchair. I witnessed these changes but refused to believe we would not be able to party again next year. The last time we visited him was Easter of 1999. At the end of our stay Danny asked Roberta and I to help put him in bed. He wanted to say goodnight since we would be leaving early the next morning and he would still be asleep. We tucked him in bed. Then he sat up and asked me to hug him. I thought it was odd at the time but I did what he asked. I did not realize until months later that he was saying goodbye to me. His body was telling him something and he knew he did not have long to go. I just couldn't accept the fact that I would not see him again, and except for the hug, I treated it like a normal goodbye. I can't recall now what month Easter was that year, but it had to be in March or April? On May 20th, 1999, I received the call that Danny had passed away. He was 55 years old. I was devastated. He was my friend. My bandmate. I looked up to him as though he were an older brother. The 10 years the doctors had given him was accurate not only to the year, but to the month!

We flew down to attend a memorial service the family gave for him. We also attended a remembrance family and friends held on Staten Island. His wife, Pat, in her own grief, went through a period of loss where she lashed out at him and only had empathy for what she went through during the ten years of his illness. People grieve in different ways. I understood her pain but found it difficult to entertain this negative energy towards my friend and the person he was. In another culture he would be referred to as a *mensch*.

Because of this barrier and for other non-related issues, about five years had passed till we were once again on the West coast of Florida. We were visiting Roberta's sister Donna, in what was then called Largo and is now known as Seminole in the Tampa Bay area. It was a Friday and I called Pat to say we would be driving past her home on Sunday on our way back across Alligator Alley (I 75) to our home in Margate. We were retired and as "snow birds," we spent the winter months in Florida. We wanted to see Pat and take her out for lunch. The next two days brought torrential rains which persisted on our drive on Sunday. We reached Pat's home on Olympia Way under a dreary dark firmament while sheets of rain pelted our car on the two hour drive. It was gloomy, slippery and foreboding as we approached the walkway. We entered the house and all the blinds were drawn. Little had changed in the years of our absence. We reminisced while catching up with all the Marsi family news concerning his six daughters and their families. Pat's youngest daughter and her son were now living there but were unavailable to join us. An hour and a half had gone by and it was time to eat. Blinds still shut, we expected to be greeted by the same weather that raged when we arrived. To our surprise and delight, the day had turned a hundred and eighty degrees. The sun was beaming and as I walked out the door I was almost blinded by the reflection of light off a penny that was lying on the ground. It was heads up and brand new! If it had been there when we arrived, it certainly eluded us. It was a remarkable turn of events. I took this as a good omen. I walked out on the street to the car and looked up to the bright sky. There was a giant arc of a rainbow above us with brilliant colors. I called to Roberta to come see this phenomena. Pat pointed out that there was not one, but two giant rainbows, one behind the other. I said to Roberta, "What could this be." My only conclusion was that Danny was saying hello to us! Like when he told me to hold him and hug him when he was saying goodbye. That's it. Danny was saying hello. Two colorful rainbows spanning the sky. One for each of us. Danny was saying hello! What else could it be?

Shark, Peter Shark & The Naughty Bird!

My friend Shark was in the business of selling marijuana. He began this enterprise sometime in the late 1960's. At first, it was a venture that encompassed friends, and was strictly local in nature. Over the years it grew and instead of selling nickel, dime and quarter pound bags within the neighborhood, it had expanded to bulk proportions where he would have hundreds of pounds stored in a warehouse in the factory building next to where he lived on Downing Street. At the peak of this entrepreneurship, he was selling huge amounts to an art dealer in Belgium, and his clients included the likes of Keith Richards of the Rolling Stones and other celebrities.

I discovered this in a startling way. In 1977-78, I was teaching in John Phillip Sousa JHS 142 in the Baychester area of the Bronx. It was located across the street from Cardinal Spellman HS. The program I worked in was a learning center for emotionally disturbed students. I liked them and they liked me. We got along well and I realized they were similar in many ways to the kids I grew up with in Greenwich Village when it was a predominantly Italian American enclave. It had many elements of a ghetto but escaped that classification due to the fact that the area was also inhabited by intellectuals, artists, musicians and various people devoted to culture, theater and education. A colleague of mine was reading the NY Times in an office teachers shared to relax between their classes. I guess it could be called a lounge but there was little respite there due to the nature and behavior of the children we were servicing. They were often brought to this space after being removed from the classroom to "cool down" after some incident that occurred with their classmates. These incidents were on going so the room was more often than not in a state of turmoil. The designation as a lounge or rest room was a misnomer.

Anyway, my colleague Mr. Feinstein, knowing I came from the Village pointed out an article in the paper that the parents of a "drug" dealer were kidnapped and were being held for ransom. It was my friend Shark's parents and $80,000 was sought for their return. Luckily, the situation was resolved and his mother and father, Angie and Paul were returned unharmed.

The bird incident happened a few years earlier when I was still living in Greenwich Village in an apartment at 64 MacDougal Street just off of Houston. Shark's business was strictly on a cash and carry basis. However, over the years, he would at times barter with a client who failed to have the full amount for the merchandise bought. If Shark liked or was interested in items they offered such as silver or gold jewelry, rare coins, pieces of ivory or jade, or any other unique specimen, he would take that as part of his payment. I was unaware, but one such specimen that caught his interest, was a large Macaw or talking parrot.

One afternoon Shark, along with his younger brother Peter Shark, arrived at my apartment with a beautifully colored bird on a stand. I was out at the moment but my wife Angela gave them entry. Apparently they placed the bird in a corner of the living room. When I arrived, several minutes later, I was unaware of the animal. I came in with a couple of other friends and we immediately struck up a conversation. Shark began to roll some joints and took out the hash pipe. We were all stoked and having a good time. Every time the talking lulled and quieted down to a whisper I heard a loud "Screw You." I looked around somewhat confused but let it go knowing we were all bent out of shape and figuring it was just someone letting off some steam. It happened several times more. I finally turned to Shark and said, "What the hell was that? What's going on here?" He replied. "Don't worry, it's just the bird." Peter pointed out this exotic green and blue parrot with large feathers in the corner on a stand. I asked him what the deal was. He told me Shark was initially fascinated by the bird and took it as part payment on some smoke he had sold. It was from South America and was worth several thousand dollars. He quickly tired of its constant chatter. The bird would only quiet down when a hood was put over its head at night to go to sleep. Peter lived on a lower floor in the same building with his brother, at 38 Downing Street. Shark gave the bird to Peter with instructions to feed it regularly and in general take care of it. Peter kept the bird right next to the front door of his apartment. The bird wouldn't shut up. Every time Peter passed the bird on the way out it would be squawking. Peter always addressed him loudly with a "Screw You", while slamming the door in the bird's face on the way out. It only took a few "Screw You's" for the bird to pick it up and "parrot" what it heard. Let me be clear, as the saying goes "Pardon my French," Peter spoke this brand of French fluently to the parrot. And "Screw You" was a euphemism for the language that he really used. Needless to say, the bird was an excellent student and his street vernacular became quite extensive. Because of this proclivity, he became known in our circle as "the Naughty Bird." I don't know if the bird is still alive. The average life for a Macaw is 60 years with the oldest known to live to be 112. Some of these birds have long lives. That parrot somehow summed up the neighborhood, symbolizing its independence, creativity and brazenness. If he is still alive, I am sure he is cursing up a storm and giving his current owners *agita!*

Nights To Remember

My friend Shark (Dennis Guglielmo) was a person of multiple interests. He was an authority on wine, health food, cannabis, weight training, diet and nutrition. When he became involved in any subject, he was not satisfied to just command it, he made sure he had an encyclopedic knowledge of it. He also knew everyone in the neighborhood and was like the unofficial mayor of Greenwich Village. He would walk around having conversations with all the shop keepers and street pedestrians. He often gave out bottles of wine to friends as associates as gifts. He knew good wine, enjoyed drinking it and liked to share his good finds with others. His largess was boundless. He routinely gave out money on the street to homeless people and the disadvantaged. This wasn't just pocket change. It added up to quite a sum on a daily basis. The primary business he was in, selling pot, decades before it became legal, was very profitable and gave him the entrepreneurship capability to invest in wine, open a guitar store (Carmine Street Guitars) and speculate in other ventures. He always had a wad of cash in his pocket rolled up into a ball with a rubber band binding the bills. Most of them were of the hundred dollar variety.

Once, I was celebrating my younger son Arden's birthday at Zinno's Restaurant on 13th Street between 6th and 7th Avenues. It was owned and operated by another neighborhood guy and friend, Bobby Perazzo. Besides having a great menu it spotlighted some of the best jazz around. We often went there to dine, listen to the music and hang out with Bobby who was a master raconteur. This evening Shark arrived late and threw a brown paper bag on the floor between us where we sat. He was always handing out joints but my two sons were not quite adult enough to indulge. They were teenagers living in Bergenfield N.J. which was a more protective environment than the city we grew up in. I asked Shark a couple of times what was in the bag. He said something green, and not to worry about it. Knowing him, I figured it was a Kilo of grass that he was going to sell. He was constantly on and off the phone so I assumed he was in the middle of a deal. Finally, he went outside to continue his conversation. My curiosity got the better of me and I reached down and opened the bag and saw it was filled with cash. What looked like a good part of my yearly salary as a teacher was stuffed in there. Shark returned to the table, ordered Champagne, and we continued the celebration.

Evenings like this were typical for Shark. He often took a coterie of people out to dinner on his treat. Roberta and I were often included in these gatherings both in the city and when he was down in his condo at the Marlboro House on Collins Avenue and 58th Street in Miami, when we happened to be in Florida at the same time.

One night he took us out to eat at Pacific Time on Lincoln Avenue, in Miami Beach. It was "hot" at the time and was one of the "in" places to be. He also invited an old Village friend Sergio Bosi who happened to be dating Elba, Roberta's childhood friend from J.H.S. They were living together in Aventura which is just north of Miami. Sergio was in business shipping and selling stereo equipment from Miami to Brazil. Sergio's mother was Brazilian and his father was an Italian who left Italy during the Fascist regime. Sergio lived in Sao Paulo and came to the Village when he was a teenager. Shark's wife Kathleen was also with us. We were seated at a table and the fireworks began. Shark knew all the restauranteurs and was allowed to bring his own wine to drink with dinner. He often carried around a large compartmental tote that held numerous bottles of wine. Shark favored the better rated wines and consumed them heartily. He always brought a bottle for the owner, manager or *maître d'*. As was his custom, he would enter these establishments wearing his ever present Guinea Tank Top Shirt. After a few bottles of wine our group became rather boisterous. I noticed that the table behind us, which sat 14 people, was occupied by the baseball player Bobby Bonilla. His current wife and children from various marriages and relationships were all present. The kids seemed to be more interested in what was going on at our table. And why not? Shark and Sergio argued in a continual battle of one upmanship, who could out drink the other, along with a litany of various challenges, boasts, brags and tomfollery. At one point, an older woman with her gray hair in a bun, approached the table. She spoke softly and was polite and dignified. She addressed the Shark: "May I ask why you are sitting in this wonderful restaurant in your underwear?" Shark asked her where she was from and she replied the Midwest. He told her people out there didn't know anything. Then he said, "Do you want to see my underwear? I'll show you my underwear," as he stood up and proceeded to unzip his pants. He was about to pull them down when his wife Kathleen interceded. I looked over at Bonilla. He looked upset that his wife, children and family were being subjected to this. I thought he might come over and there would be trouble.

Shark never wore a suit or tie and could not be mistaken for a "made" man like John Gotti replete with silk suit, pinky rings and swanky leather shoes. But he had the looks and demeanor of a tough guy who could possibly be a henchman, enforcer or head cracker for the mob. He wasn't any of those things. He was a shrewd street wise highly intelligent kid who had made his own path. This impression, of him being something other than he was, often kept people from interfering in his business. Luckily, things quieted down and we were able to finish our meal without incident.

Another evening in Greenwich Village will always be remembered. Another old friend, Gary De Vincenzi, owned and operated a 5 star restaurant located at 50 carmine Street called *Cent'Anni*, which is Italian for 100 years. This expression is used as a blessing to wish people a long life, or as a toast while having a drink. He employed top notch chefs and the food was unbeatable. He had a long success but this evening was at the end of the run for the restaurant. An old friend of Roberta's, Ray and his wife Michele, met us for dinner at Zinno's. Ray had worked in South America and the Caribbean while living abroad for many years building non-profit homes for indigent people. He was a clean cut, straight laced idealist with high morals and sensibility. After dinner we decided to walk south to the part of the Village I grew up in. While walking down Carmine Street we happened to look into *Cent' Anni* and saw Shark sitting at a rear table holding court. We went in to say hello and were immediately ushered to the back table and given seats. Gary sat down with us and the fun began. Shark promptly questioned Ray about his cash flow. It seems he was looking to sell grass to him. The last thing Ray wanted to do was buy weed or smoke a joint. They cleared the table and the wine started to flow. It appeared that Shark and Gary were trying to best each other in the next bottle we would sample. Shark took out from his tote a 1975 Bordeaux that he had paid $700 a case for, the year it came out. This was the late 1990's and that wine was now priced at $28,000 a case. I complimented Shark saying what a good investment he made. He could sell them and gain a huge profit. He lamented he would if he could, but he already drank most of them.

He had a temperature controlled vault where he kept his collection. I believe it was located either on 14th Street or 23rd Street and his space was adjacent to the famous restauranteur Alain Ducasse. Gary went into his stock and picked another excellent wine to sample. Each new wine was accompanied by a new glass. Meanwhile, Gary had instructed the cooks to be creative and serve some appetizers. They responded with New Zealand mussels with pesto sauce, bruschetta with tomatoes and herbs and tangy shrimp. They continued to bring out a variety of delicious delights. Pretty soon there was no room left on the table for anymore glasses. The evening was getting late and we had drunk a lot of good wine. Gary, being the owner, and knowing the place was on its last legs, brought out the *coup de grace!*

When the restaurant first opened almost 20 years prior, Vincent "the Chin" Gigante had given this bottle to Gary as an opening gift and as a good luck gesture. "The Chin" was the *capo* of the Genovese family. He had access to swag and other goods beyond the reach of the common man. The bottle was a 1905 Madeira. In those days wine was shipped across the Atlantic Ocean and because of the length of the passage neutral grape spirits were mixed in to preserve the wine. Aside from that, how many bottles of this vintage could still be in circulation? They brought out another set of fresh glasses, uncorked the bottle and poured some into each glass. There were six of us at the table. It took several minutes for the sediment to settle to the bottom of the glass. To this day, I don't think I, or anyone else at that table, ever tasted a smoother or more delicious wine. We savored it then and remember it now as one of the great nights in the Village. Shark, Peter Shark and Gary are all gone now. I miss them and will always remember my good friends, that naughty bird and those unforgettable nights! That bird may out live us all?

Carole Canecchia

Fire Escape Window

The window off the fire escape was indeed an escape into adventure! My first cousin Lillian's apartment was in the back of the building and the view from her window was of the beautiful gardens that separated the brownstones on Barrow Street. It was quite lovely and a respite from the relentlessness of the city. Nothing took place there except for an occasional sighting of a blue bird or cardinal or of someone watering the flowers in the gardens.

Things were different at our fire escape window. I could see all of the action on the street: kids playing ball or roller skating, workers from the factory across the street delivering their merchandise, pottery classes going on in the Greenwich House Pottery, street musicians serenading the populace. I particularly enjoyed the accordion players coming up and down the street. What a show!

Amusements for children growing up in the 1950's was minimal. We had TV with Howdy Doody and Kukla Fran & Ollie being very popular but programming time was limited. Aside from card games, Monopoly, pick up sticks and jacks and reading, there was little to occupy us.

We were stuck in the apartment for what seemed an endless period. The polio epidemic peaked maybe around 1952 and my mother would not let us go out and mingle with other children. My outlet was looking out the window. I was drawn to a window across the street at 14 Jones where a couch was placed right in front of the window. A couple were lying next to each other and kissing for a very long time. Then the man began to take her top off. I became increasingly upset as I saw the female protesting vehemently. I wanted to watch but thought this might be something I should not see? I was both frightened and stimulated by this display. I thought I should leave the window but could not tear myself away. I was curious as to how this would play out. They kissed, he fondled her, she protested. It went on like that for a while. Then he attempted to pull up her skirt and take her panties down!

He seemed to be arguing with her and it looked like he grew angry. Finally, she jumped up from the sofa and they both disappeared. I was eight years old at the time. I was so relieved. I did not want to see anymore or know the final outcome. I still remained curious, looking out at their window, from time to time, but the couple never appeared again.

A Push Cart

My mom cooked simply not having too much money to spend on fancy food. Our meals were peasant style unless we took home leftovers from a family feast or our neighbor Frankie Papa gave us an occasional steak.

The pushcarts were very colorful and prevalent in our neighborhood. They stretched several blocks from 6th Avenue to 7th Avenue on Bleecker Street. These carts brought the daily necessities right around the corner from our tenement homes.

I don't remember my mother venturing beyond the cart located on the corner of Jones and Bleecker. That cart was filled with fruits and vegetables with signs that read 2 cents, 5 cents et cetera. It is still, to this day, very vivid in my mind.

On day my mother was counting out her change to pay for her provisions. It is possible she was a little short. The Italian owner of the push cart, Pepe, accepted whatever she could give him and told me to pick out a nice piece of fruit for myself. I was delighted and felt so very special.

Just A Shove

It was just a shove
Down the steep
5th flight of our tenement
Must have been provoked
By my younger brother.
Still it haunts me
What did he say or do?
To make me put him in such danger?
Except for his tumbling down
I cannot remember if he was hurt
Or if I was punished?

Linda Canessa

Papa Didn't Preach!

I guess I was about 14 or 15 when we used to go to Saint Anthony's dances on Friday nights. We decided, in all our wisdom, to have some scotch instead of the beer we usually consumed before we went to the dance. (Big Mistake!)

I was slow dancing when I started feeling unwell. I told my partner, "I have to throw up." I went to the girl's bathroom and passed out.

The next thing I can remember is sitting on the toilet and my girlfriend Yolanda telling me the priest called my home and my dad was coming to get me. She kept drilling in me to say we went to Johnny Santoro's house and had a little wine and got sick. My head was throbbing and she kept drilling me.

My father arrived and he would not even talk to me. He walked in front of me all the way home. Not a word was said.

Michael Carbone

Greenwich Village Vignettes-Continued

I met Al (Butch) Canecchia about 15 years ago after he published the original Greenwich Village Vignettes. It turned out, we only lived two blocks apart in Riverdale, Bronx. I vaguely remember him from his days hanging out with Sharky. We've become good friends since, and he has mentored me in his love for high quality pizza.

The title of my story is sort of a homage to the original – it captured so much of our shared neighborhood experience and my intention is to add a few more memories.

I used to do a routine for those I didn't know, about our neighborhood, especially those who thought their life, let's say in Columbus Ohio was ideal. "There is the universe, our solar system, planet Earth, the USA, Manhattan and the Village – center of it all!" Never sure if they got it. The exact center of the center, for me, was two square blocks bounded by Houston Street, Spring Street, Thompson Street and Sullivan Streets, where I grew up. These events occurred at least 50 years ago, but I remember them as vividly, as if they happened today.

I truly feel we were blessed to live the "golden age." Post WW II NYC, the Village as our playground, and a sense of everything being either available or attainable.

I left my house one morning for work about 7 am, or so, it was still dark, I think. In front of me totally unexpected was the Feast of St. Anthony in all its 1950's glory. Actors milling around in period costume, the feast improbably in full swing. They were filming the famous scene in the Godfather II, where De Niro goes from rooftop to rooftop and back again, to kill the local Don. I always waited for this scene and pointed out all the places I remembered, whenever watching the movie. The really odd thing was, I didn't think it was unusual, as I had become used to our neighborhood getting lots of attention.

Me And "The Chin"

My dad was born where Minetta Lane meets Minetta Street and my mom at 106 MacDougal. They met and married and lived at 112 West Houston for the rest of their lives.

He never bothered with high school and when his parents moved to the Grand Concourse, he refused to go. Instead, he stayed behind with my great grandmother, who spoke no English, and his two doting aunts. He did one lucky thing in his life and that was to marry my mom – a great cook, with infinite patience.

He was a truck driver and my mom was a home maker, most of her life. He was also an unlucky gambler, which meant, he always owed money. One time he must have gotten in over his head and couldn't pay, so he decided to go on the lam. This, for him, was lying on the pull out sofa bed in our living room, while trying to figure out his next move.

The doorbell rings. Before we could answer or ask who it is, bounding in, is the youthful, crew-cutted Vincent G. He comes in with a smile, very respectful to my mom, and then sits across the table from my dad and begins talking street code. I am old enough to understand. Basically, Mr. G. is telling him, all is okay. He just needs to come out and they'll figure something out. No need to hide. Message delivered, my dad is relieved. Mr. G. takes his leave as respectfully as he came in.

For years afterward, if I was ever asked if I knew Mr. G. (as by now he had become famous) – I'd say, "oh yeah, I know him well. We even had him over the house." It never failed to impress.

My dad's luck finally changed. He won 12 K from the parish lottery and retired from truck driving. He took a job working for a local bookmaker working the phones. He was not allowed to gamble so he finally made some money working in gambling. Go figure.

· · · · · ● ● ● ● ● ● ○○○○○○○ ○ ○ ○

Lorraine Catalano

There's No Place Like Home

I grew up in Greenwich Village on Cornelia Street in the time period, 1950's – 1960's. I attended Our Lady of Pompeii School right across the street from my parent's apartment. With only one parent working, there wasn't much left over, but to my parents, a Catholic school education for their only child came first, and the tuition was always paid. School uniforms were hand me downs from a neighbor's daughters. Lunch in the cafeteria with the other kids was too expensive for our budget. Grandpa Bastiano's house was right across the street so I would go there lunchtimes and eat with my family before returning to class. Most all the other kids ate at school. I can't remember exactly what age I was when one of the nuns told me I couldn't continue to do this and that I had to eat my lunch in the school cafeteria with the rest of the kids. Why was I so different? By the time I reached Grandpa's house for lunch that day I was crying. When I told my mom what happened, she and Uncle Charlie were upset. But that was nothing compared to Grandpa Bastian's reaction. His face got dark and scary. "They no want you come to Grandpa's house? *A Matsada!* (I will kill you) meaning he would kill them! Grandpa proceeded to pull up his suspenders and get dressed to go confront the nuns. Mom shouted, "Pop, pop, no! Sit down. Forget It." Grandpa continued to curse in a mixture of Italian and English. It took a while for him to calm down. We never went to talk to the nuns and I can't remember exactly what happened as a result of the events of that day. I continued, as usual, to have lunch with my family at Grandpa's house and not at the school cafeteria. Grandpa was mostly a quiet man and rarely smiled. I was afraid of him and found out later I wasn't the only one. But my Aunt Mary defied and stood up to him. It wasn't pretty. There was verbal and physical interaction between those two.

The nuns were hard on us kids. The boys in all my classes were usually the ones who got in trouble and would be punished in front of the entire classroom. One time, one of the boys had to wear a piece of chewing gum on his forehead for the whole lesson, because he had been chewing when it wasn't allowed. I was a shy, sensitive kid, whose feelings were easily hurt. I wasn't popular and at one time was considered odd because, as an only child, I invented characters to play with. I had a broad imagination which wasn't appreciated by the other kids and certainly not encouraged by a parochial education. It took me years to realize that my school days at Pompeii are what groomed me to be a responsible worker and to follow the rules (sometimes more rigidly than others).

My parents were also strict and often I wasn't able to do things the other kids did. I remember some days looking out the window and seeing my cousins and other neighborhood kids playing on my block. I believe they meant no harm and just wanted to protect me. As a kid, I did not understand any of this.

Every Sunday we went to mass, whether you liked it, or not. You dressed up. That meant no jeans. I had to use a bobby pin to hold my little veil in place on my head, as all girls were required to do.

I remember as a young teen, hanging out on the steps of Pompeii Church, on the corner of Carmine and Bleecker Streets, with my group of friends. I started not wearing my glasses during that time, because I began to notice the boys and I wanted to look cool. Sometimes I was labeled a snob because I didn't immediately say hello when someone approached. This was only because I couldn't make out who it was unless they came close by or spoke to me.

It was our neighborhood, our little world. You couldn't go a block without seeing someone you knew (sometimes that was annoying.) How I wish for those days now, where it looks like everyone you see is a stranger because they all look the same. I miss hearing our unique NYC accent. Today when I hear that accent in a crowd my head turns around with joy. This doesn't happen too often, unfortunately. Our neighborhood was safe and rarely did someone get out of line, and if they did, they soon had a change of heart. My family, my friends, my little world was Greenwich Village. Neighbors were always around to help like an extended family. We trusted each other. We knocked on other people's doors just to say hello, how are you? When the weather was nice the neighbors socialized by setting up lawn chairs right outside their apartment buildings. It was impossible not to notice everyone's comings and goings. Most times, I felt safe and protected, surrounded by people who knew me and my family from birth. It was hard to get away with stuff when you knew someone was going to tell your parents in a heartbeat that they just saw you doing such and such. To my parents, going across 6th Avenue was considered entering another neighborhood, and was not allowed without being accompanied by an adult. Later on, in my early teens, I began befriending kids from the East Side. I felt proud and excited to say I knew these kids, but my parents weren't thrilled. The East Side neighborhood was too far away for them to monitor me. I went there anyway.

    We had plenty of stores, supermarkets, grocery stores, fruit and vegetable stands. Everything was fresh. Our mothers cooked at home and we rarely went out to eat. You sat at the family table to eat and God forbid if you took a book to the table to read!

    In an effort to appear independent, I moved to Brooklyn for a short period of time in my twenties. The grass seemed to be greener but I was very disappointed and returned back to my parents' apartment. I had found, that like Dorothy, in the Wizard of Oz, "there's no place like home." Today, decades later, I am still living in the same apartment I grew up in. I have seen many, many changes. I love each street of my neighborhood. They hold so many memories, both good and bad, which I relive as time passes by. It's difficult to accept some of the changes. The loss of the small mom and pop shops that were forced to close because of competition from large chain stores. The Specialty Shops that closed because internet shopping took over. Restaurants have sheds outside extending onto the side walk, making it difficult for pedestrians. Many parking spots for cars have been lost due to bike lanes. Sadly, Our Lady of Pompeii School, my alma mater, closed last year. Condos are being built around the whole area and more and more people are moving into them. Many of these people are transient, they stay for a short period, then make way for the next short term tenant. It's hard to get to know them. The massive amount of people is becoming overwhelming. No familiar faces or smiles.

I remain close to a few people who grew up with me in the Village. We share stories and memories. Whenever I go away, I am comforted when I return to the neighborhood. No matter what, I will always love Greenwich Village!

Anthony DeCamillo

The Crying Knish Man

When my son Daniel was a boy, I maintained a common parent-to-child tradition, handed down from my dad to me, recounting experiences of the "olden days." Imbedded in these recollections was an observation or theme that could be absorbed and valued over time. Often these little vignettes carried some ethical or moral principle. They were the Greenwich Village equivalent of Aesop's Fabless now falling on the ears of neighborhood kids hungry for guidance and a glimpse of what might lie ahead. I often fashioned them with intriguing or exotic titles like, "The Indian Man Who Worked with Wood," "When Grandpa John Made Me a Sword," "The Day Roy Rogers Said Hello" and "The Crying Knish Man."

I grew up in the West Village, at a time when pizza from coal-fired ovens was only sold in whole pies. Patches of old cobblestone and a few remaining fruit and vegetable horse-drawn carts were about to vanish from the streets. Popping up throughout the day was a "man" for everything – the celebrity hawker's woven into the neighborhood's communal fabric: "The Watermelon Man," "The Italian Man," "The Whoa Peaches Man," "The Ice Man," "The Knife Sharpening Man," "The Horse-Ride Man," "The Knish Man," "The Jelly-Apple Man," and "The Hot Dog Man," to name some of the more enterprising. What follows is the story of "The Crying Knish Man."

When the 3:o'clock school bell rang at Our Lady of Pompeii,

a common midday sight was of kids rushing out for snacks. That usually meant heading for options across the street. A lemon or chocolate ice from Rocco's pastry shop or a sugar-rush of choices at Harry's candy store were classic favorites. Another popular choice was the tempting treat of the knish man. The degree of excitement for this simple pleasure seemed out of proportion to his humble set-up: a make-shift metal cart with multiple slide-out trays of potato knishes heated by coal or gas from below. A stack of small brown bags, waxed paper and a tin salt shaker, completed the whole operation producing these warm, crusty munchies.

One afternoon, coming from school, I noticed a different person tending the cart in the usual spot, at the corner of Carmine and Bleecker Streets, across from the church. He was an older man in worn clothes, apparently not yet comfortable with either the job or the location. Nevertheless, he began filling orders for the hungry munchkins who encircled him, with mothers gathered close by. Soon a situation emerged that would cast a shadow on that bright afternoon.

A young policeman approached the knish cart, and after looking it over, began to question the old man. Despite language limitations, the man's feeble attempt at speaking and gesturing, somehow managed to communicate his circumstance. He conveyed to the officer that he was new to the area and just learning the trade. After a few more exchanges, the officer, speaking and gesturing with authority and determination, pulled out his thick leather violations pad and began writing a summons.

All activity abruptly ceased. A silent gloom hung on the space as the crowd sensed a shift in purpose and power. The man obediently stopped working, took the ticket, looked it over, and lowered his head. Forlorn and staring downward, he placed both hands on the cart handle as if to steady himself. Slowly, tears fell silently on his hands and the cart as he tried to recover from the weight of what just occurred. Instantly, one mother gingerly approached and attempted to console him. Through gentile sobs, he explained his desperate situation and that it would take him days of work to pay for the summons. The kids reflexively mirrored a collective sadness for this man and their own loss. The mother, as if transforming energy from the old man's grief, seamlessly turned to address the cop. "You know this is going to take him days to pay?" said the woman. "Lady, you're supposed to have a permit for this," the cop fired back. "He doesn't have one, it's the law." The woman parried, "Yeah, I understand, but he's new here and doesn't know all the rules yet." Hanging on her last word, the officer rebuffed, "That's not my problem, it's his, the law's the law." Just then a collective swell of sympathy seemed to emanate from the group of mothers listening, as if inheriting a communal problem. It was like the instinctual response to hearing a baby's shrill cry, or an emergency's rush to action

One by one, the chorus of moms edged closer to the policeman, surrounding the cop, the kids, the old man, the cart, and the aroma of all those coveted knishes. What was now unfolding felt similar to the surge of possibility as a movie hero comes galloping or swooping down closer to the action, in order to save the day. Eyes widened and ears perked up in the front row of this popcorn moment. To my surprise, each mother contributed to a litany of what might be called the "yes, buts." "Yes," another mother chimed in, "But look at how this is turning out for everyone." Shifting to her, the cop retorted, "Again, not my problem, I have a job to do." Then another mom: "Yeah, but he's got a job to do. Where's the harm here?" The policeman, now sensing a maternal ambush of sorts, swung around and said, "Look ladies, there are regulations," he pleaded. A new mom shouted, "Okay, but are you always aware of every regulation?" The cop stiffened, "Lady, the law's the law." And a voice from the crowd. "Really officer, are you creating more of a problem than fixing one?" The chorus continued unrelentingly. "What about the spirit not the letter of the law? Every judge would know about that." The policeman now feeling his authority being overshadowed began to plead, "I can't do anything about it now, I already wrote the ticket."

And then from another inspired mom, the *"coup de grace"*: "Yes we know, but things can happen to tickets, they get lost, damaged, mistakes are made on them." The officer, with the round of 'Yes, buts" still echoing in his ears, glanced over at the chastened old man, then to the hopeful eyes beaming on the children's faces... and Bingo! This contagion reached the officer's deeper nature as his spirit seemed to slip out of his uniform and to form a complete circle of hearts. As if now compelled by a higher purpose, in a highly uncommon gesture, he took the summons out of the old man's hands, and tore it up.

I don't remember if I even had a knish that day. Probably did. But what I can vividly recall is how easefully, how eloquently and effectively those neighborhood mothers, through their naturally protective stance, could model what a collaboration of care looks like. What child or adult does not have a place deep within, held dearly for a mother? Maybe it's one reason why we use maternal references, like "Mother Earth," to capture the tone of that original nurture. If the tears of that old man and the mother's response had an impact, it was to remind us of who we really are, and how, at any point in our lives, we can compassionately become part of something larger than ourselves.

· · · · · · ● ● ● ● ● ● ● ● ● ● ● ● ● ● ● ●

Paula DeNicola

Greenwich Village, My Magical Kingdom

You never knew what you've got till it's gone. Truly. Growing up in Greenwich Village in the 1970's I yearned to live elsewhere. Upon visiting after moving away, I learned how lucky I'd been, and sometimes I wish I hadn't left.

People are in complete awe upon discovering where I'm from. I read in David Patterson's *The Last Days of John Lennon* that John wished he'd grown up in Greenwich Village, and I'm amazed. But my upbringing must have inspired me, as I used the Village as a backdrop in my latest novel, *Penny's Song,* based in 1970.

Now, it seems like a dream. Did I really walk on Bleecker, Thompson, Sullivan, Perry, Downing, Gay and Carmine Streets, quite possibly among the likes of Bob Dylan and Joni Mitchell?

Did they really perform at The Bottom Line, Terra Blues, The Bitter End, and Café Wha? As I walked near those clubs, a plump eleven year old in a Catholic school uniform and laced black oxfords?

The Washington Square Park live music, poets, acrobats and artists seemed a nuisance then, obstacles, as I trudged by on the way to someplace I no doubt took for granted. Now, I hunger for these things, rarities in central New York State, the place I presently call home.

We lived at 169 Sullivan Street from when I was eight months old until I was six. It's interesting that I remember every inch of that apartment, especially the kitchen, where I sat daily, eating the middle out of every single loaf of prized Italian bread my mother brought home. I blame the size of my thighs on that, perhaps the only real bad memory of the Village, since I never got to wear mini-skirts like my friends did!

Oh, that inimitable aroma of freshly baked bread! Walking to school as a kindergartener at ST. Anthony's, the scent soothed away my worries about Mamma and Pappa leaving me for the day. My new friend, Antionette cheered me as well. When it was time for her to hide during "hide and seek," she placed her hands over her eyes. Hysterical!

Once I stood outside St. Anthony's School in a minor panic until my older brother, Fred, arrived. My folks were unaware of the half day. As adults, Fred retold a scary story. For reference, we lived on the top floor of a five-story building, around 75 feet from the ground. I was three or four, sitting on the windowsill, legs outstretched and hanging out as he watched from school, helpless and panicked. He said when he looked back I wasn't there; he hoped I'd gone back inside versus the alternative.

Fred and I shared the love of baseball with our Dad, Franco. Being somewhat oppositional, I preferred the Mets over the Yankees. Fred, who people said resembled Robert De Niro, considered himself a frustrated baseball player. He used to take my dark pink rubber Spaulding balls for stick ball and never return them. They're probably all still on some roof somewhere, along with my memories.

We subsequently move to 13 Carmine Street, Apartment 12, just prior to my father's passing. I lived there with Fred, our mom, Anna, our sister and Francesca, born after my father passed. I'll always remember every square inch of that "railroad" style apartment that ran straight from the kitchen to the living room, and our downstairs neighbor, Marguerita, who we tortured with noise. I recall my father's brown Naugahyde chair in which I sat every night, doing homework, listening to music on the stereo cabinet that also housed those precious glasses my mother got for free with green stamps.

Another windowsill mishap occurred on Carmine as our cat, Katy, decided to lunge at a passing bird and fell four stories to the concrete. She lived and stuck around until 1979.

Along with painters, writers and performing artists, Greenwich Village boasted some unsavory types who contributed to some of my most vivid, comical moments. Yes, some of them appear in my book. The guy who always strolled through Father Demo Square who one day had stuck cigarette butts in his nostrils; the woman who hit me with a carton on Bleecker Street as I waited for my mother to finish shopping at the butcher's and fresh vegetable stands, shouting, "Get outta my way!" The guy who climbed the statue at the peak of Our Lady of Pompeii Church, shouting, "Hey, hey!" I hope he made it down safely, as I had off that windowsill. And the guy who showered in the rain under a tree. In the interest of sensitivity, I'm sure these people had mental health or addiction issues. Meeting them was like foreshadowing my future, as I later worked with individuals with special needs.

The seventies also meant the advent of the Hare Krishna people. Once, while I listened to the long version of Chicago's song, *Beginnings*, with a lot of ending percussion, my mother ran to the window, and in Italian expressed her disdain for the Hare Krishnas, who, she thought, were back. They weren't, at least not at that moment.

I'm saddened that many of the stores I frequented growing up, among them Zito's Bakery and Nocetti Hardware, are gone, as are their proprietors. In some cases, the original shop names remain etched above the doorway. I'm elated that House of Oldies on Carmine, where I purchased my first 45s: *Layla* by Derek & the Dominoes and *I Saw the Light* by Todd Rundgren, still stands. Murray's Cheese and Matt Umanov Guitars, which my husband loves, are still around, as is the Feast of St. Anthony.

As a girl, I'd always eye the marquis on the Waverly Theater to see what played. I saw *Serpico* there, the first movie I attended independently with my new H.S. chums Maryanne, Lidia and Joan. The price of a ticket then buys you a coffee today.

I loved the little library on Morton Street, where my best friend Barbara lived. I was fascinated by the Jefferson Market Library, its castle-like elegance sprouting up in between the little streets, among the shorter structures. Greenwich Avenue at 8th Street is a pretty section. I treasured shopping on Eighth Street between 6th Avenue and Astor Place, where I picked up all the latest cool fashions and first learned about "head shops." The Riviera on 7th Avenue, where my neighborhood friend, Daniella and I sat in 1983 dreaming and scheming to start a film business, Reality Productions.

My family liked using the roof for entertainment and as a reprieve from life, way before it became chic. As I said, what I failed to appreciate then, I reminisce about with fondness now. Whenever I smell fresh tar I'm transported back to that roof. Glancing down at the 'greenery" I mistook as palm trees I later discovered were sumacs, I imagined being in Florida. And the Pan Am building reminded me of the airport. I always wanted to get away, didn't I?

Ah, the roof, where we used to sunbathe and watch the fireworks on the Fourth of July. We have a ton of graduation roof photos. I used to write up there. Once, I had to use the toilet. We had a shower in the kitchen, but the toilet was outside the apartment in the hall. Returning to the roof, my mother told me some of my pages had blown away. *"Che?"* (What) I never ran faster than I did back down those stairs, out of the building and into Father Demo Square, where an older man read them.

"Excuse me. Those are mine. They just flew off the roof." "Oh, well it's very interesting," he replied. Apparently, he enjoyed my autobiography as told from the eyes of a sixteen-year old!

I attended Our Lady of Pompeii School, across the street, from first grade to eighth, where I met so many fantastic people who are still my friends to this day, in particular, Barbara and Sal. Reading the elementary school primers, with John, Jean and Judy boarding a school bus, only served to increase the longing in me to live among trees and ride a bus to school.

I attended St Joseph's High School, where I met up with Antoinette again. I couldn't believe she had changed so much. Sister Martha glared at her when she walked, skirt waistband rolled up, clomping in her platforms, head held high. Still shy and quiet, I looked up to her.

Sadly, years later, I heard she'd passed away. All good things must come to an end, as both St Joseph's H.S. and Our Lady of Pompeii School closed. The former closed in my junior year, 1976, and the latter, in 200, as a result of the Coronavirus pandemic.

But I met my best friend Lidia, with whom I'm still in touch with, at St. Joseph's, and we attended Cathedral High School as seniors together.

Lidia and I rented an apartment in Kew Gardens, Queens, in the spring of 1980. We returned to the Village to live in her parents' residence at 118 Christopher Street when they moved to Portugal. I loved that small, cozy adorable place! Lidia and I shared bunk beds! And we had an interior bathroom.

I have so many fond memories of Christopher Street: One of the first Gay Pride Parades, our house parties, and one of the first exotic bakeries across the street, where my friends and I got Lidia a birthday cake, embarrassing her, and making her take pictures with it!

Lidia moved to Portugal in the fall of 1981. I moved to Ellenville, N.Y. two years later. I was transformed into a tourist visiting Greenwich Village. I learned to appreciate the wonder, the fascination, as an outsider looking in, especially through the eyes of others who experienced the Village for the first time. The wide-eyed looks on my kids Richie and Alice as they recognized streets, restaurants, and stores from movies, the excitement in my friends' voices as they chose a café, and in my mind, knowing I'd always lived among these places but never ate there. My son Logan will never forget playing chess with a guy in Washington Square in February 2020. The moment was worth the five-dollar gambling loss. I treasure the photos I took of Logan and my youngest, Reese, in the same spots I frequented as a child in Washington Square Park. And what's now known as the Playground of the Americas.

People ask me why I left, with obvious envy, as they tell me they cut school and hopped buses and trains from Westchester or New Jersey to visit the Village. I can only think of the ambitious Paula who'd always wanted to live in a house, not an apartment, with a yard, surrounded by birch and willow trees, not crowds. But do you realize how many dreams I've had of walking through the old neighborhood since I left? How many times I dreamt about Pioneer Supermarket, and discovered my brother had too? I now live on the Oswego River, clean, adventure filled waters. But I long for my old neighborhood and the lower Hudson River at the piers, teeming with litter but immensely inspiring.

Yes, the grass always seems greener on the other side. In my case, I really believe the concrete was better than the grass in ways only a Greenwich Village native can understand. And you never have to mow it!

Paul De Paolo

64 MacDougal

My Pompeii classmate Al Canecchia moved into 64 macDougal in 1968. Before the space was transformed into an apartment it was a grocery store owned by Mr. Chelcia. I guess we were about 12 or 13 when my friend Bobbie Bonacchio and I had a part-time after school job there. We worked for Mr. Chelcia sorting soda and beer bottles in the basement.

At some point we decided it was too much work. We devised a plan where we would sort one case then throw the bottles from the second case over the wall where they were hidden behind an oil tank. We did this on a consistent basis, one for real, and one over the top of the wall. We couldn't believe we were getting paid for this!

In the same basement there was an old coal shoot and coal storage area. Bobby and I decided to investigate. We went back there and soon after we started to itch like crazy. We found out when we got home that we had gotten fleas. Another exciting time with Bobbie.

My friend Roger Segalini was dating Rosemary and we became friendly with her brother Jerry. Jerry was painting his father's candy store, so we decided to help him. After we were finished we all went to Leroy Street Pool. We climbed the fence and with a bar of soap we all washed up in the water. Fun times.

In conclusion, I must thank Rocco for saving me from drowning in the boy scouts and in the Hudson River. Exciting childhood.

Kathleen Firth

The Starfish/Just The Friend I Needed

As the factory whistle blew, Veronica wrestled to get their one overly stuffed suitcase on board the train as her husband George embraced his younger sister Ethel and said "goodbye." This was one of grandma's stories about the past and how my family came to New York City. My grandmother reminisced out loud, "We almost missed the train and Ethel got docked for 3 hours for being late. I can still hear your grandmother scolding her for coming to this day. Poor Ethel, she worked at that place until she died."

Long before they were known as grandma and grandpa, or even mom or dad, George and Veronica had decided to escape what they saw as a dull existence in the stoic and cold New England Milltown in which they were born, to seek different opportunities.

George had saved money from the advertisements he had done for the local burlesque shows. A skinny little guy with the scars left over from a terrible case of acne – he was not suited for factory work. Veronica, just as lean, towered over him, at 5'11, but it seemed as though they never noticed. Orphaned at 14, my grandmother worked at the local laundromat.

Together they raised just enough money for a couple of train tickets and headed to the big town. Within a couple of days, they found an apartment in Greenwich Village. Now I am very certain my grandparents did not intend to stay in that tiny apartment for the rest of their marriage. Two children, six grandchildren, and several great and great, great grandchildren later – 72 Barrow Street, Apartment 2B, had become their forever home.

It was in this little section of New York City called "Greenwich Village" that runs from 14th Street to Houston Street and stretches between 5th Avenue and West Street, that they would find themselves surrounded by others from all over America and the world, who came in search of opportunities and acceptance they would never find elsewhere.

On a beautiful Sunday in February of 1938, Cynthia, my mother, was born. It was a big deal in the building because there were not a lot of children being born during this time because of the war, which changed the world on so many different levels – some seen and some not yet apparent, but the rules of the game were being rewritten.

As a native Villager, I have often wondered why the Village attracted so many artists, musicians, poets, intellectuals and political activists. Was it simply because, just like all the other suckers, they got off the boat or train and found work and cheap housing here first? It seemed like that to me from just knowing some of the history of my own neighborhood. It is a well-known fact that the local bars where my grandfather hung out, like the White Horse Tavern, that poets like Dylan Thomas, liked to hob knob with the local longshoremen.

Growing up in the Village, it was not uncommon to meet celebrities, especially in the 1960's when I went into adolescence.

Mom and I lived with my grandparents, along with my aunt and her 3 children. I was born when she was barely 17 – my family told me that my father was a handsome Latin who was more than happy to just leave my poor mom alone to fend for herself. As a single mother, she struggled with raising a child on her own and simultaneously trying to find a life of her own.

My grandparents were more Celtic than New England and were adopted very quickly into the large community of Irish families in the West Village. As a part of this extended family, my young mother could not get away with anything. In fact, our big extended Irish family reported everything she did to my Catholic grandmother. She looked for an apartment, but even in the 1950's and 1960's, affordable housing was hard to find, in part due to the gentrification of the neighborhood, along with the growing influx of NYU students and their friends.

It was a big day for me and mom when someone told my mother about an apartment on 15th Street and 8th Avenue. Just a block above 14th Street. The place was a real find – it was everything we ever dreamed of.

I loved my grandparents, but I was going to be 13 soon, and I was not allowed to leave the block without receiving the 3rd degree from my grandmother, who intended to double down on this girl. Trust me, I found my freedom, but nevertheless, I was more than thrilled to move and get as far away from my grandmother's grip and the eyes of the old church ladies from Saint Veronicas, Saint Josephs, and Pompeii – yes, they had a network!

Now there would be nothing but adventure for a girl child on the streets of the Village in the late 1960's with a working mom who had a life of her own and my grandparents out of the way. Now the streets were mine.

Now I may have been 12 but I looked older, partially because I had inherited my grandmother's height of 5'11", but also, I was very gifted with the makeup. My wardrobe consisted of a box of clothes I found in my grandmother's closet that contained a lace corset and a large hat with a black veil and feather. My corset looked nice with the tight faded jeans, and the black veil complimented my red lipstick. I was artistic, and like many of the young people of my youth, I expressed my creativity in colorful fashion.

There is a little secret that is not discussed very often, and that is that many of the children growing up during the sexual/drug era in Greenwich Village, were not protected. In fact, we were preyed upon by the waves of people who came to our neighborhood to do what they could not do elsewhere – this is part of the reason why I was not a virgin at 12. Sounds horrible nowadays, but many of the Village kids simply fell between the cracks of the world's changing social mores and the breakdown of the American family after World War 2. With the new drugs that were hitting the streets and the universities, there were just no rules.

That spring and summer, when I was not running all over the Village, I spent my time "stoop sitting" and observing the characters on my new block. It was a great street, and I got to know everyone quickly. Johnny's Bodega was next door. He was very cool and knew everything that happened on the block. Johnny had a fancy Cadillac, and he came and went as he pleased. Everything about him smelled good, like the leather of his black jacket that matched his dark hair and the rims of his glasses. I often wondered if Johnny owned the house of prostitution in the building two doors down, but I never asked. The old Puerto Rican men on the block would turn the garbage cans into percussion instruments by turning them upside down and banging on them till dawn on Friday and Saturday nights. These gentlemen were so talented they could make music from mud. One day, one of the drummers explained to me how in Puerto Rico the landscape was very hilly, and that the rhythm of the music reflected the landscape of the island. In fact, he informed me that an educated ear would be able to tell from which part of his tropical island the song originated from just by the rhythm alone.

The fire hydrant was full blast on hot days for many of the other kids on this block and me, this was heaven on earth. My new boyfriend was the super's son and he was four years older than me. To be accepted on the Street it was a good idea to have a boyfriend. However, at 12, I was not at all serious about being in a committed relationship or much of anything else. My favorite night of the week, was Thursday, because my boyfriend played basketball with all the other jocks on the block – they were gone. Also, my mother usually worked late on Thursdays – so I was alone.

One of these nights, as I was sitting on the stoop, a tall handsome man walked towards me from the direction of 8th Avenue; I had never seen him before on the block and he introduced himself as the *'Prince of the Night."* I liked him instantaneously because he liked to wear costumes like me. Mostly he wore a blue velvet jacket and a white puffy shirt. However, I seem to recall he also wore a light brown leather fringe jacket, which I was gearing up to ask if I could borrow.

There was a slew of pedophiles and geeky guys that walked around the Village with guitars and cameras asking girls, "Would you like to be my model?" The guys with guitars would try to impress us with cheesy songs. But this guy was not trying to impress me. We just connected somehow.

I was a wild child, but I was not attracted to drugs. That was something that tourists came to the Village to do. I had also seen the effects of these drugs on family members and friends, and I had no intention of losing my mind or self-control, because as fun as I thought the world was, I was familiar with its darker side as well. In revisiting this part of my youth, it is odd that I connected with him at all because he was tripping! However, The Prince of the Night did not scare me. Knowing myself, I can be honest and admit that I might not have been doing drugs, but I was right out there with him. That summer, we sort of had an unspoken agreement to meet each other on Thursday nights on my stoop.

My name is Kathleen, but he called me Katherina, and although he loved me, our relationship was not sexual at all. I wondered if it was my innocence that drew him to me? For the life of me, I do not remember what we talked about that summer. He mostly rambled on about places and characters that he assumed I knew. I had no clue so this made him even more mystical to me. Sometimes I thought he was having a conversation with someone else that I reminded him of. I vaguely remember him showing me some written papers and a sketch. He always seemed to have something up his sleeve and I knew he looked forward and/or depended on meeting me on the stoop that summer. Just a kid, I placed him to be in his mid-twenties. Once I saw him when the sun was setting, he looked to be older, or maybe just sad and tired. It was at this moment I realized how lost he was. In my heart, I knew we were two wounded doves, and it was his vulnerability that made him special to me and made it possible to overlook the drug use. I cannot count the times he came that summer. If he did not show up on one Thursday, he would magically appear the next. If I had to categorize him, I might say he was a uniquely beautiful man, or perhaps otherworldly.

Now that I am 65, I can tell you that I have never connected to many people in my life. This connection, however, was real, but not to be long lasting. One night my perfect stranger came to the stoop and told me he had something special for me. He took a starfish out of his pocket and asked do I have a glass bowl to put it in. I invited him upstairs to our apartment. We walked up the five flights of stairs in the tenement building. I opened the door, and we went into the kitchen, where I found a glass bowl. He filled it with tap water and placed it on the table. Then, the Prince of the Night pulled out an electric cord, which looked like he had cut from an old lamp, and severed it in half with a razor blade he had in his pocket. Then he attached the spliced electrodes to the starfish's legs.

After the Prince plugged in the electric cord, he signaled for me to hold hands and submerge the starfish into the bowl filled with water. I quickly said "no." I was not scared because I knew that somehow this was a compliment, but I was not ready to die from electrocution.

He looked embarrassed and immediately walked through our apartment and out the door. I remember him slipping away down the staircase, and I knew I would never see him again. I never intended to hurt his feelings. He was a tender-hearted person. But, I also did not want to meld into him as one, or be some sort of virginal vessel into Atlantis.

A few years later, I went into the High School of Art and Design, a public school for artistic kids. This is where I noticed that many of my classmates were carrying around sketches of my friend. I told somebody in the cafeteria that I know that guy. They looked at me with an odd expression and said," That's Jimi Hendrix. He is dead. You can't know him." Teenagers in my H.S. started wearing T-shirts with his face on them. I learned that he was considered by many to be one of the greatest guitarists in the world. He never played for me – we were just friends. He was just as scared and alone as I was, and I will never forget him as one of the best friends I ever had. He was just the friend I needed that summer, and friends like that are hard to find.

In later years. And with the birth of the internet, I learned that Jimi Hendrix did have an apartment around the corner from where I lived with my mom. I am not certain if the year was 1968 or 1969, I have never been good with time. Here are a few lines from one of his songs, I believe it is called, "A Merman I Should Turn to Be" "Hooray, I awake from yesterday. Alive but the war is here to stay. But my love, Katherina and I decide to take our last walk through the noise to the sea not to die but to be reborn. Away from a life so battered so torn. Forever, forever."

Now was I the Katherina in these verses? I doubt it because I also found out on the internet that he had a girlfriend named Kathleen; perhaps he called her Katherina too? I will never know. I do know that we shared a time and that we were both on a path, and we connected in a special place called Greenwich Village.

• • • • • • • • ● ○ ○ ○ ○ ○ ○ ○ ○ ○ ○

Dennis Genovese

Father Albanese & The Little Girl

When I was ten years old my mom put me on the list to sing in the Amato Opera. I didn't want to and I never sang before that, as well. Anyway, I enjoyed it when Tony Amato would praise the group and tell us how wonderful we sang and sounded.

Carol Ann Zuar, my first girlfriend, who happened to live in my building, sang with me, also. After two summers I quit against my mother's wishes. I couldn't take the old ladies who removed our makeup after each performance. I now think back and realize how stupid that was of me.

So, I made a deal with my mother to sing in the church choir. One day, upstairs in the balcony of Our Lady of Pompeii Church, the choir was practicing and being briefed on some technicality. Father Albanese, the pastor, walked over to me and lightly slapped me in the face. "I don't know who put you in the choir Genovese, (pronouncing it Genavezzy,) he said, because you can't sing!" I wasn't hurt a bit and when he stepped away a little girl next to me said, "I think you sing good." She was trembling with fear. I answered her with an angry, "I Know."

I thought about this incident twenty years later and felt like a real jerk. I didn't mean her any harm. I was just responding to the so called priest. I'm sorry I caused hurt to the one who consoled me. I should have thanked her for her compliment. Tony Amato gave me confidence to sing and a person of God, who should have been a healer, tried to take that confidence away. It took me fifty years to address it. Whoever that girl was, she is my heroine.

Frankie "Mouse"

Somewhere around 1969, the group the Roman Numerals began to disband. Butch, (Al Canecchia) was the first to leave. With his education and career in danger, he had the most to lose. It was a four person family with tears coming from all of us, including John Marsicovetere and his younger brother Danny. We were all at Emilio's Tavern having a few beers and talking it out. The group remained together for another two and a half years. Johnny, Danny and I, tried to go on with three wheels, one wheel missing. Finally, in 1971, the Roman Numerals were finished. John became a born again Christian and moved upstate to Hadley, in the Lake George area. Danny would leave Brooklyn and settle in Staten Island working hard to provide for his family and fronting a band that played at weddings and other affairs. Butch received his Master's Degree which secured his teaching license in the N.Y.C. Public Schools. Over the tears and decades to come, we would produce a swell of his compositions and mine, in conjunction with Karen Mantero and the Fallen Angels, and solo work of all three.

During the last year that the four of us were together as the Roman Numerals, we performed at a dive on W 3rd Street called The Purple Onion. It was run by a couple of low level hoods. We eventually wanted out of the contract when the goons ordered us to show up Christmas Eve to perform. They threatened us and told our manager, Elaine Sorel, that if we did not sing at their club on Christmas Eve, we'd never sing again! Elaine was crying in fear.

Johnny called his older brother Frankie on our break and told him of the situation. About an hour or so later, close to midnight,

Frankie "Mouse" pulls up in a cab. The two nasty wanna be made men immediately transformed into respectable gentlemen. I said, "Hi Frankie, great to see you," and we hugged. The two club operators who were "Al Capone-ing" us, suddenly were shaking in their pants. "Oh Frankie, we're sorry, we didn't know they were your brothers," as they trembled in fear.

As we were leaving, I asked Frankie to wait for us because one of the bouncers was giving me a hard time. He was on the make with one of the Go-Go Dancers that were performing next to me on stage. He didn't like the fact that we were close to each other and she was smiling at me and giving me the eye.

Frankie said, "Don't worry Dennis it's all okay." We finished loading our car with the guitars and amps and left.

When Danny was driving me home I asked him who Frankie was working for. He reluctantly told me he was a hit man for Crazy Joey Gallo. My mouth dropped. Is that where the nickname "Mouse: came from? Frankie "Mouse," Johnny "Mouse," Danny "Mouse."

Within a year and a half I was gone from the group. Johnny and Danny tried to persevere. They both ended up one night at Gallo's haunt, a joint on Court Street in Brooklyn. Danny said it was a scary nightmare as the low class hoods were all over their wives or mistresses. Frankie brought Danny over to meet Joey Gallo and told his brother to kiss his ring. Danny said, "What? I'm not kissing any ring. Get out of here." Joey told Frankie "It's okay. He doesn't know about our traditions."

AS they were leaving, the same hoods who searched their guitar cases for hardware when they arrived, hassled them again as they were leaving. A year or so later Frankie "Mouse" was convicted of putting the hit on another mobster in a bar on Thompson Street. He served over twenty-five years in prison before being released.

Frankie is alive and well today. He will forever be my big brother, who saved my ass. I love him as I do Johnny, Danny and Butch.

Dominick Joseph Genovese

Growing Up In Greenwich Village

My parents and I lived on 6th Avenue between Bleecker Street and Houston Street. Originally, we lived at 264 6th Avenue in two rooms of a second floor walkup. The rent was $12 a month. Then we moved to 270 6th Avenue, fifth floor walkup. We had three rooms and the rent was $62 a month. My dad had a fit. He thought this was too expensive. My grandparents lived two buildings away on the fifth floor. We used to go over the roofs to see them because the buildings were attached. Nobody locked their doors because everyone felt safe. IT WAS THE NEIGHBORHOOD!!! Across the hall from my grandmother lived a man named Marlon Brando, before he became famous. You would also see Bob Dylan, Jimmy Hendrix, the Lovin' Spoonful, and others in cafes or walking down the street before they were well known.

I used to play on my block with Richie Alba, Ricky M. and others. We played stoop ball, punch ball and softball in Houston Street Park. All we needed was a Spaulding ball and a broom stick. We made scooters out of milk crates and 2 X 4's with one roller skate. We painted them different colors and decorated them with bottle caps.

When spring came around. And the weather got warmer, we knew summer was coming and that meant NO SCHOOL! I hated School! I went to Our Lady of Pompeii where the nuns were a little crazy. They used to hit you with a ruler on your hands and knuckles. I didn't get hit much because I was shy and quiet. When I got to the 6th grade, I said, "You're not going to hit me anymore." I never got hit again.

On Bleecker Street there was a candy store called Harry's where we bought lots of penny candy and comic books after school. Right next to Harry's was Paul's Shoe Store. It was a small store with boxes all over the place, but he knew where everything was. My mother bought me a pair of PF Flyers there. Then came Keds white sneakers. They lasted a whole year.

Back then, 6th Avenue was a two way street. Now it is called the Avenue of the Americas. If you didn't make it across, there were white triangles called safety zones where you would stay until the light changed and you were able to get across.

Along Bleecker Street, between Carmine and 7th Avenue, were push carts selling fresh fruit, vegetables, fish et cetera, where people would shop.

When I got older, my parents opened a pizza store called Village Pizza. It was on Carmine Street close to the intersection of 7th Avenue South, next to Luke's Gas Station & Garage. The pizza store became a hang-out for a lot of the local kids. I worked there during this time doing different things such as making dough, delivering pies, etc. My uncle Sonny, whose nickname was Happy, got his name because he was always in a jovial mood. The two monikers got combined and eventually he was referred to as "Sonny Hap." I guess he was happy from all the beer he drank? He and I were in charge on the weekends while my parents went to Atlantic City. A slice of pizza and a drink cost $0.25. Johnny "Mouse" and "Ziggy" were mechanics at Luke's and they would stop in and sing for us. They were really good. They had a record out under the name Marci & the Mates. My father put it in the jukebox and it was regularly played by the teenagers who hung out there.

When I went to H.S., my friends from Brooklyn and Queens couldn't believe that I lived in the Village. They thought it was just for tourists. No, it was the neighborhood. Many memories.

I met my wife Antoinette (Cookie) in the 4th grade. We have been married 52 years. We have two children and three grandchildren. I can go on for days, but I will end here.

• • • • • • • • ● ○ ○ ○ ○ ○ ○ ○ ○ ○

David Hunt

Uptown Came Downtown
My Time In The Village

I was from the opposite end of Manhattan Island, a blue collar, slightly red necked neighborhood at the Northern end of Manhattan called Inwood. Famously dubbed "Ginwood" by Walter Winchell because of the proliferation of bars and saloons, not restaurants, saloons!

It was September of 1969 and I had just enrolled for my sophomore year at the new Fordham Liberal Arts College at Lincoln Center on 60th Street. I would need a part-time job to keep my head above water as I continued with my education. In those days, all colleges had a Student Placement Office to aid students seeking part-time work while attending school. We all seemed to be in need of that service. These were minimum wage jobs paying $1.25 per hour.

Posted on the bulletin board was a waiter's job in Greenwich Village, only 20 minutes south via the #1 train. It boasted $2.50 an hour! I was hooked.

In early September 1969, I emerged from the Sheridan Square Station and walked one block north to the corner of 10th Street and 7th Avenue South. Giant gaslights hung on the 7th Avenue side and the décor was "Roaring Twenties," red and black. I was expecting a world of Bob Dylan, Dave Van Ronk, and Gerde's Folk City. Instead,

I got a world of tourists and underage college kids, drinking way beyond what would be considered responsible, today. This was not the Village that I had anticipated but it was certainly fun, too much fun. I had found a home at "Your Father's Moustache," a beer and banjo emporium.

The camaraderie of the staff at "Your Father's Moustache," led to lifetime friendships with many. They all scattered all over the country but some still stay in touch to this day. (Thank you Facebook.) One young man, probably 25 years of age, had already graduated with a Master's Degree from NYU, but still lived in the Village and worked one night a week, simply for social reasons. He had a rewarding daytime job but used his part-time job to enhance his social life. He knew the restaurants of Greenwich Village inside, and out. Monte's on MacDougal Street was the best for homemade red sauce (gravy to some,) the chef was off on Tuesdays at Tetley's on Carmine Street, but the substitute made the best Zabaglione. The Ninth Circle kept bringing delicious Zito's bread and unlimited salads. Thursdays at the Cedar Tavern, upstairs under the skylights, was the Prime Rib Special. Both Fridays and Saturdays, after working till 3am, you made sure to get into Chumley's at 86 Bedford Street before they locked the doors and continued serving past the legal 4am limit. Sundays introduced me to a completely new concept – Brunch, at The Sazerac on Hudson Street.

In a matter of months, I was a *bona fide* Greenwich Village resident; sharing a luxury apartment at 3 Sheridan Square, a modern (not villagey) high rise, with a doorman. To help meet the monthly rent, my roommate and I ran poker games two nights a week. We took a percentage of the pot.

There were other games being run throughout 3 Sheridan Square, but ours was small time and we only payed off the doorman to let our "guests" come upstairs. The other arrangements were different. The tenants would be approached by the Superintendent on behalf of "neighborhood guys," and the monthly rent would be waived if the tenant agreed to be absent for a 24 hour period every week. This allowed for a Sunday game, a Monday game, et cetera. All these games in the same building but in different apartments.

My friends were college students from Fordham, NYU and a host of day hopping campuses in the Metro area. Through the bars and restaurants, I also made lifelong friends with young people who were raised in the Village. Irish mostly, from the western reaches of the Hudson River, Italians from just east of 6th Avenue, but parochial, nonetheless. St Veronica's, St Anthony's (Ant-Knees), St Joe's and Our Lady of Pompeii. It seemed the private school kids didn't need part-time jobs, but I would encounter many of them later in the neighborhood saloons like Jimmy Day's.

What I didn't know at this young age, was that the Village was really an extension of Little Italy. My new found neighborhood friends, Italian or not, would guide me to the local stores for specific items. There were some things that you simply could not purchase in International Supermarket (Later Gristede's) on Sheridan Square.

After the luxurious # Sheridan Square ran its course, I became the illegal sub-letter at 16-18 Charles Street. A non-working fireplace, exposed brick walls and a small studio space with access to a backyard garden for $89 a month. Later, a new girlfriend, would require a larger (slightly) apartment and we moved into 26 Perry Street, where I lived until marriage (a different girl,) and off to the suburbs, mortgages, two cars, the whole nine yards.

The girlfriend who I rented the apartment with was a Greenwich Village born and raised Italian American who knew the Village from that Little Italy perspective. Through her guiding vision, pasta only came from Raffeto's, mozzarella from Joe's Dairy, bread from Zito's (she knew what time was best,) and sausages only from Faicco's It took hours to shop for a simple meal, but it was all from "the neighborhood." LiLac for chocolate and Zampieri's for her favorite treat – Riviera toasts.

Rocco John Iacovone

Physics 101

Saturday and Sunday were always the best for riding our bikes. Side streets had virtually no traffic and the route we used to get to the pier was always empty.

The piers on the Hudson River were abandoned and left to ruin. I guess by now the ships were loading and unloading in Red Hook, Brooklyn, and the ferry that once ran from Pier 42 to New Jersey had gone defunct. The only thing left were the rotting empty terminals and the pilings that jutted out in the shape of the pier.

That was great for us. We could go there and play and horse around and there was no one to bother us except for an occasional couple who were trying to get a little privacy.

I used to go there alone and daydream how I'd build a raft like Huck Finn and travel down river to the ocean and I'd be off on an adventure. At low tide, you could see the gravel and sand bottom, and at high tide, the water was about 6 feet, or so deep, right where West Street met the river.

This particular Saturday, Tommy and I decided to race to the docks. The one who gets closest to the edge of the water before braking wins!

Ok. I'm ready. I know I could beat him easily but I'm going to run away with it and leave him in the dust.

Down Vandam Street past Varick, Hudson, Greenwich and over

to Houston was the path we took. Then it was just a left over towards the water. I turn to look and he's almost a full block behind. Now, I really turn it on. The river is in sight and I pick up speed checking once more to see where he is. I'm way out front. The edge is coming up fast, and I remember the scene from the movie "Rebel without a Cause." I'm no chicken, I'm cool, like James Dean, so I keep on pedaling. I get right to that very last couple of feet of blacktop just before the big wooden beam that delineates the pier from the water and I get ready to jam on my brakes, allowing only a few inches so I could swing the bike around to the right and look real suave.

Wham! I stand on my brakes for full braking power. The bike hits the wooden beam and to my complete surprise and astonishment, I fly, 5 or 6 feet into the air, just as graceful as a swan! I realize the bike was on the ground, I was in the air and headed for an unexpected swim. It struck me funny. I started to laugh very hard as I involuntarily did a double somersault in the air. I hit the salty water laughing so hard that it was difficult to catch my breath. I landed on my feet with a thump, like Superman, and felt the soft sandy bottom of the river. Now, still laughing, it was my goal to stand straight up, look around and wait for Tommy to appear. He did. As Tommy looked with cautious curiosity, the expression on his face sent me into another bout of laughter. He didn't know what to expect. He was happy that I was okay. We both had a good laugh before figuring out how to climb up and out. With his help, I climbed the 8 foot wall. We laughed more about what he thought happened, and what was I thinking? We hung out until my clothes dried. It was my first real physics lessen.

I still remember the stench of my clothing!

Summers Were Hot

In those days, summer was hot, winter was cold, and spring and fall were nice. Spring with all its promise gave way to summer and fall which had a way of getting us excited about winter coming with all of its snow.

Second week in June and it was hot. The St. Anthony feast was going strong and this meant two things: we knew where we would be hanging out for the next 10 nights and that mentally, summer vacation had started, even though we still had a couple of more weeks of school.

After walking the length of the feast up and down a couple of times, we all decided to head for Leroy Street Pool. The outdoor pool had just opened up. It was a big pool with one third of it dedicated to deep water and diving. It had 2 diving boards. One was about 3 feet above the water while the other was about 12 feet above. Some of the older, tougher kids, used to dive off the roof of the gymnasium building, which was adjacent to the pool. The height was about 2 stories high. One part of me wanted to try it, but the other part said it was too dangerous and scary for me to even climb out there and attempt such a stunt. I remembered a story my father told me about when he and his friends used to swim down by the docks in the Hudson River.

Those kids, the real tough kids, used to dive from the top of the pier loading structure, which was a good 4 or 5 stories high, into what was only 12 to 14 feet of water at high tide and 6 to 7 feet at low tide. The rivers were dumping grounds then and heavy metal containers were used to haul milk. These containers were about three feet high with a diameter about 14 inches wide with the neck and head just a bit smaller. One day a kid dove from the top height and never resurfaced. After much chaos and confusion, with his friends frantically looking for him, the rescue team found him with his head stuck in one of those milk containers. I used to swim at those piers too, but I never ever dove into any waters that I didn't know after hearing that story.

Back to Leroy Street. It had an indoor and outdoor pool. The indoor pool was where I saved Paulie's life, and I may be the only one who knows it, but that's another story. Memorial Day weekend was the official opening of the outdoor pool. Among others, Jack Dempsey, Jake LaMotta and Rocky Graziano used to hang out at this pool. Dempsey was there every day and the others would drop in with friends every now and then. We loved that pool.

Now here we are about 10 of us and we are intent on swimming. The pool is closed. It's probably after 10pm but that makes it all the more exciting. On the Leroy Street side, we get to the 8 foot fence of the park and climb over it. A short jump gets us onto the roof of the rest rooms. A careful walk up and over the peaked tin roof gets us to the other side. Hang down, jump, clothes off and it's a race to see who's first and last in whatever it was we were doing.

We had a great time swimming, then some other kids join in, and we are playing around like it's a Saturday afternoon. All of a sudden, shouts echoing, "It's the cops. It's the cops." Now our guard is up and I look around. Everyone is scrambling to get away. It's out of the pool, clothes on, jump toward the fence, as legs go into pants. Get shoes on, decide which way to go, while everyone skedaddles their separate ways. The easy way up the fence is crowded. I chose the Clarkson Street way. It was the deep water side. The fence was much higher there, but there were fewer kids, and I had no time to lose. It was time to go. Up and over, not even looking and coming down the other side. I'm thinking I'm home free while hanging from the fence and ready to jump to the sidewalk. All of a sudden, WHACK! It's a nightstick across the back of my legs. I let go of the fence and hit the floor. That whack took away any muscle control I had. Other kids were getting away, while I had 2 big blue uniformed cops smiling at me.

"So out for a nice swim. This is serious business. You broke the law, son. You're in trouble now." Then to his partner who caught another kid, he said, "Whadda ya think they do downtown with these juvenile delinquents?" "Throw the book at em," he replies, "This is breaking, entering and trespassing. They're getting awfully tired of these kids."

They had me good and scared. We're in the gymnasium lobby now. Never thought of it but there must have been a night person there who called the cops. They'll tell my mother and father. I'll get a JD card, they'll never let me in H.S. and I'll be marked for life! My parents will be heartbroken and I'm through. Finished. I'm washed up at 13. But how'd this happen? I'm thinking I'm not a bad kid while the back of my legs are hot and aching.

I saw a little softening in the older guy's face. He must have seen something in my face. "Would you rather come downtown or should I call your parents and tell them?" "No, don't tell them. Please, I'll never do it again. We were just playing around. We didn't do anything wrong. Please, I never did it before and I promise I'll never do it again."

They went outside while we waited. We waited about an hour. Sweating the whole time. It looked like the older cop called the shots. I was praying at that point and on edge for what seemed like hours. "Ok. We decided to let you two go. But if we ever see you doing anything again, we'll run you in. You understand."

"Yes sir, yes sir. Thank you officer. We'll never do it again." All of a sudden, I was out and free again. Freedom is a wonderful thing. You don't even know how wonderful until it's taken away, even for a short time. Even though my legs hurt, I walked home thanking those cops for that lesson.

I never did it again.

• • • • • • • ● ○○○○○○ ○ ○ ○

Robert Leake

Call To The Local DJ

I wrote to a local DJ about an older cousin of mine who had a local Village band in the 1960's, "The Roman Numerals." They were slated to appear on "The Ed Sullivan Show," but Bobby Kennedy was assassinated just before the performance and the entire show was preempted for coverage of the event. They did get to play in Carnegie Hall before that but their big shot was lost when TV spot was cancelled.

The Street I Lived On

The street where I grew up in Greenwich Village in Lower Manhattan, N.Y.C., was called Jones Street. It was a unique street one block long. It was wedged between Bleecker Street and West 4th Street. While growing up in the mid 1950's and early 1960's, my block was between the old world and the modern world. When I was a young lad, Bleecker Street was the Italian neighborhood shopping area that offered Italian specialty shops selling Italian delicacies. The smells of fresh bread from the bakery, cheese store, pork store, olive barrels and pastry shops were incredible. The soda shop sold soda from the fountain mixed with syrup and seltzer water (you could add vanilla, cherry or other flavors) if you wanted. An egg cream consisted of chocolate syrup, milk and seltzer water, stirred to perfection, till it had a creamy, malty froth. This was my favorite. These shops served their own homemade Italian ice, lemon, chocolate or strawberry. They were the best I ever remember having. Our local pizza joint only sold pies, not slices. The coal fired ovens made the best pizza, which is hard to find anywhere else. Pushcarts would roam the streets selling fresh fruit, vegetables and fish. I still remember my Great Aunt throwing down from the window, a few coins wrapped in a tissue and telling me to purchase various items. She would haggle over quality in Italian, but understood what she was yelling down from her apartment window. After, the vendors would park the carts on Bleecker Street, which would line the block from 6th to 7th Avenues. There, they would continue selling their merchandise. At this period of time, ships docked in Lower Manhattan along the East and Hudson Rivers. They brought fresh items which the pushcart vendors would daily load up on. The term Fruit Vendor, was on my Great Grandfather's Immigration papers.

On West 4th Street, at that time were Beatniks, musicians and people from the art world. The shops there sold leather goods, clothes and had several "head" shops. This area was more *avant garde* and considered more artsy and bohemian. Musicians would stop on the corners and play their sometimes strange looking instruments. I would see organ grinders with their monkeys holding tin cups, hurdy gurdies, and steel drums. One gentleman in a suit would set up a long case in the shape of a portable organ, place drinking glasses with water in varying amounts, and use a spoon to play tunes by banging the glasses of water. Before playing, he would tune the glasses by sipping water from each glass until the amount in each glass was just right to produce the pitch he wanted. I was fascinated seeing this at a very young age. Then in the spring, West 4th Street became a mecca for artists selling their paintings. This was an annual tradition that I believe may still be going on?

My block, was on the cover of Bob Dylan's 1964 album "The Freewheelin' Bob Dylan." My apartment, at 11 Jones Street, is the first building on the right that has a fire escape, in that photo on the cover of the album. The first building on the right without a fire escape was a statue factory that made marble statues for the churches. I would roam inside with my bicycle, watching with fascination, the giant marbles coming to life, only to get chased out by the foreman, whose name was Danny DeVito. He would be in his glass booth yelling, "out, out, you sonnama _____." With a flick of his head and a raise of his eyebrows, the stone mason standing on his stool, hammer and chisel in hand, would signal me to leave through the garage sized door. During prohibition, my grandfather owned a speakeasy on the second floor above the statue factory. When dating my wife in the 1980's, there was now a bar where the factory stood. The bar owner still had marble pieces on his wall wondering where they came from. I was able to fill him in. The speakeasy story got me drinks on the house! My building, plus the other two buildings, adjacent on the right, with fire escapes, is where most of my family lived. As a child, I still remember playing and visiting with family. Very few locked their doors in those days. The smell of the meat sauce coming from my great aunt's apartment was like heaven. Her "gravy' was started on Friday for Sunday diner. A piece of fresh bread dunked in the gravy was the prelude to a Sunday feast.

Just past the fire escaped buildings on the street was a stable that housed NYPD police horses. My great aunt's apartment window was just about level with the stable roof. My older cousins would make the short leap from the apartment window to the roof top, to retrieve rubber balls that were hit there from the stoop ball games being played on the street below. The lowest building on the left side of the street was The Greenwich House Pottery, a community recreation center and art studio. Kirk Douglas lived on Jones Street when he worked at The Greenwich House, well before he was a famous actor. My dad volunteered at Greenwich House and remembered working with him. A friend of mine was Bob Dylan's super when he lived in a brownstone on MacDougal Street between Bleecker and Houston streets in the Village.

Carla Lewis

I Know How Great It Is!

I have always been proud to be a life-long, brought home from the hospital, resident of Greenwich Village. My parents, Teresa and Carlo, were originally from Rockaway Beach, Queens. They lived across the street from each other on Beach 81st Street. My father, fortunately, played basketball, and on scholarship, attended Fordham College, with room and board included. He really enjoyed his time on campus in the Bronx.

My parents married while my father was in army service. My mother worked in Manhattan and commuted on the LIRR. She had a position at a realty company, which made it possible to find an apartment she liked. Teresa found a treasure in Greenwich Village on Morton Street. When my father returned from WW2, he spent several months on Staten Island at an Army Hospital for severe head wounds. After being discharged, from both the army at the hospital, he arrived at 52 Morton Street.

C.J. (my father's moniker,) was happy to start back to work. He rode the "tubes" as he referred to the PATH to New Jersey. He liked the idea that the ride was a reverse commute. The train was much less crowded and he did not have to drive a car.

He became very upset when they told him he would have to move to Sandusky, Ohio. It was an unpleasant surprise that worried him. General Motors had decided to close its offices in N.J. and

Connecticut, and move all staff to Ohio. I was in College at the time, so I was able to remain home. My mother had to learn how to drive, followed by my father. My younger sister went to Ohio with them and would eventually learn how to operate a vehicle.

After the family settled into Sandusky, it took my father almost a year to get with the program, to fit in, and have a good time. Change is very hard. Daddy finally felt at home enough to join the Mid-West life style: bowling, driving to malls and visiting historical places. Ohio has produced 8 presidents and my family has visited all their residences.

My mother joined Welcome Wagon, first being the visited, and then, being the visitor. She enjoyed helping newbies get settled. Teresa was quite a socialite and had athletic strengths as well. At least once a week, she and her buddies would hit the links to get some golf in, then move on to chat and have lunch with her compatriots.

When we all lived on Morton Street, which is still a very beautiful and mostly unchanged block, we would always look west. Weather permitting, we would be treated to a colorful sunset. Sometimes, my mother would go down from our apartment to the sidewalk to fully view and enjoy the event. Now, if she happened to call when the sun was going down, she would give a description of how it looked in Sandusky.

I caught her love for sunsets, and when it's possible, I try to make sure I'm able to catch one. When I do I get the feeling she would have enjoyed it with me.

I am lucky to have also enjoyed many fun activities from my life in Greenwich Village. These include: dances down in the basement of Our Lady of Pompeii, nowadays senior classes at the Greenwich House, practicing for CYO swimming races at Carmine Street Pool, making candles in the Girl Scout meetings at St. Luke's, eating great pastries on Bleecker Street (there were three), buying fish at the stores on Bleecker (there were three), attending movies at the Waverly Theater and meeting friends at the Hudson Library to discuss interesting books we had read, just to name a few.

I still live in this wonderful, arty, intriguing, unique and world famous hamlet known as Greenwich Village. The name and place shows up in movies, plays, books and television. Unfortunately, it has been remapped and shrunken in size by realty moguls. Now, some of us live in the newly invented, West Village.

I still get the same response when someone asks, "Where do you live." I respond, "In the Village." They say, "How great it must be." I answer, "I know how great it is."

• • • • • • • • ● ○ ○ ○ ○ ○ ○ ○ ○ ○ ○

PHOTO GALLERY

Arturo's Pizza

Basketball Team 1

Basketball Team 2

The Bomber Boys

BomberBoys

Bon Soir

Cafe Figaro

Cafe Wha

Carmine Street Pool

Cherry Lane Theater

Downing Street Park

Faicco's

Folklore Center

Gaslight Cafe

Greenwich House Pottery

Greenwich House

Johnny, Bobby & Gill

John's Pizza

Judson Memorial Church

Manny's

Murray's Cheese

NYU

Ottomanelli

Pompeii 1956

Pompeii 1957

Pompeii 1958

Pompeii 1968a

99

Pompeii 1968b

Pompeii 1968c

Pompeii Church

Provincetown Playhouse

PS8

Raffetto's

Richie Havens and David Noferi (a.k.a Tony Orlando)

Rocco's Pastry

Roman Numerals

Sheridan Square

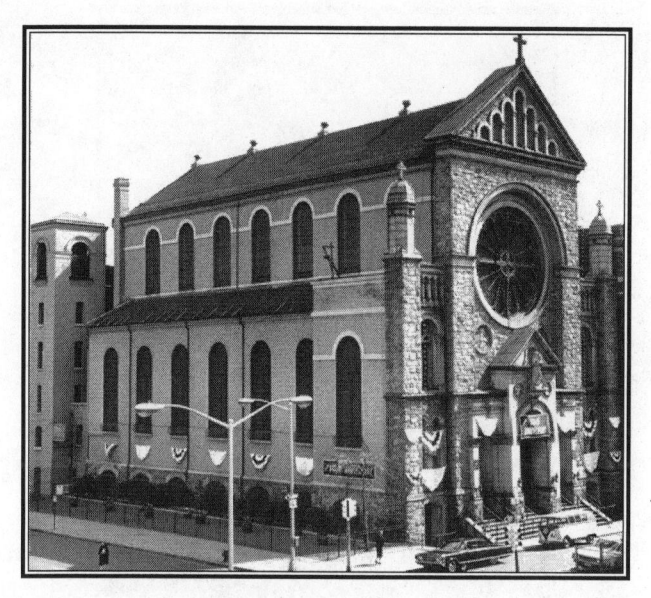

St. Anthony of Padua

St. Joseph's

St. Veronica's

The Bitter End

The Purple Onion

The Village Gate

107

The Village Vanguard

The Youngtones

Tiro e Segne

Triangle Club

Trude Heller's

Waverly Theater

White Horse Tavern

Zito's

Richard Lorraine

Growing Up In Greenwich Village

My family moved seven times while I pursued my career, and one of the usual questions that was asked when we met new people was where we were originally from. I would answer that I was born and raised in New York. Of course, to me New York was the city. No, not all the five boroughs of the city, just Manhattan. Most people would then ask another question like, "Were you born upstate somewhere like Rochester or Syracuse?" That's when I would tell them that both my wife and I were born and raised in Greenwich Village. Most people thought that hardly seemed possible given the reputation of Greenwich Village and the news stories that came out there. That's when I begin to reminisce.

Back then, the Village, as we called it, was full of lower and lower middle income families. With the price of real estate in the area today, the vast majority of those families are gone, replaced by Hollywood types, bankers, hedge fund managers and other wealthy people. When I was growing up, the south side of the Village was primarily Italian families, while the north side was predominantly Irish. I lived on Barrow Street, which was kind of in the middle.

Then other questions came up like, "What did you do as a kid living there?" Well, there were no organized sports to speak of when we were young, no Little League baseball, Pop Warner football and the like. At that time, I'm not sure I knew what golf and tennis even were. So what did we do? Easy answer, we went out and played in the street, no adult supervision, just the neighborhood kids. We played two kinds of stickball, one with a manhole cover as home plate and the other where home plate was chalked on a wall. We played with a pink rubber ball that was stamped with the manufacturer's name, Spalding, a major sporting equipment company. For whatever reason, we all called it a Spaldeen. They cost a quarter at the time which was not insignificant. If a Spaldeen was hit on a roof or a fenced-in alley, we always found a way to go retrieve it. If it broke a window, we ran away. Sometimes the ball rolled into a sewer opening, which was a disaster, and most times was the end of the game.

We played a lot of other street games as well. Chinese handball, ring-a-lerio, stoop ball, roller hockey with a roll of black friction tape as a puck and many others. Somehow we had sports seasons, which seemed to just happen. We'd play one game a few weeks, then suddenly move on to another. We were rarely bored.

As we got into our teens, we left those games behind and began to expand our horizons. Our world was the Village, and it extended from 14th Street south to a few blocks blow Houston Street in the area now known as SOHO. The west boundary was the Hudson River and the east boundary was 5th Avenue. East of 5th Avenue was generally called the lower east side. There you found Italians, Chinese, Jewish people, Hungarians, Ukranians, Poles and other ethnic groups.

At that time, we never heard of an area called the East Village. Being older, we began to discover other things the Village had to offer. Unfortunately, drugs was one of them. As I got into my teens, marijuana was prevalent, but for too many the primary drug of choice escalated to heroin. I can, but won't make a list of the friends and acquaintances who died either from an overdose or from the violence that surrounded that culture.

I was not attracted to that lifestyle. Instead, I was attracted to the mostly dark haired, dark eyed Italian girls. The only downside to that was most of them were good Catholic school girls. Kissing, hugging and dancing the fish to the slow songs at St. Anthony's dances was okay, but for most of them, not much else went on. In fact, kissing after midnight on Saturday was considered a sin because the girls would be receiving communion that Sunday.

I met my beautiful Italian girl when I was sixteen years old. At St. Anthony's she asked me to dance with her when a ladies choice came up. I told her I didn't dance and she turned and walked away. A little later, as the dance was breaking up I saw her with a boy who was all set to walk her home. That was a really big deal back in those days, and meant that you liked that boy or girl. I realized my mistake, went up to them and announced that I was walking her home. Lucky for me she said yes. We don't remember who that boy was, or why I didn't get a punch in the face at the time, but sixty years later she's still my girl and I couldn't be happier. Also, she's gotten over that no kissing after midnight thing.

This is about the point where people, despite being fascinated with the stories, would begin to get antsy. It was time for me to signal the bartender for a drink and ask about their background and how they arrived at the same place as us. Next to ours, most of their stories were pretty pedestrian and couldn't begin to compare with the experiences and sometimes craziness that we lived "back in the day," growing up in the tumult that was Greenwich Village in the 1950's and 1960's.

John Marsicovetere

My Life In Greenwich Village

I was born in Greenwich Village on March 8, 1941, at Christopher Street. In those days, there were apartments in the back of family owned shops. I happened to be born in the back of my Dad's shop called Coral Upholstering. My family consisted of three girls, three boys, my mother, father and grandmother. My grandmother, Big Mama, was a retired medical doctor and delivered at least four of us in that exact apartment. There are many facets to my life that shaped who I am. I have always loved music. Yet, my family and I always knew there was something more, something bigger than myself that I was always searching to find. Many of my stories involve my life in music, hard work, challenges I faced growing up in a poor Italian-American home, and the good people that influenced me, and God. I'd like to share some of the stories that made me who I am today. First Memories:

I was around three years old, and my family and I were all together in front of the store. Air raid sirens were sounding in the distance. This was a warning to turn off all lights. The only light permitted was a small red light about the size of a Christmas bulb. All curtains were closed on the windows and the city was in total blackout. These were air raid practices all during WW II. There was a feeling of fear in the room, I guess that's why I remember it so well.

Another early memory was also at about three years old. It was a horrific event. I remember my grandmother tripping over me with a basin of water. She was running to put out a fire that had started in my Dad's shop. My grandmother was no small woman. She stood over six feet tall, and when she hit the floor there was a loud bang. I did not know it at the time, but my older brother, who was about five years old, started the fire. He was playing with matches under the table in my Dad's shop, and this is where the rolls of cotton were stored. When he lit a match the book caught on fire. He got scared and tossed them. They landed in the cotton rolls and the fire quickly spread. Cotton is saturated with oil to preserve it, which caused an instant blaze throughout the shop. I remember standing across the street, everything was smoldering. Later, I was told my older sister, Ann, who was eight years old, saw the fire from the corner and ran home to grab my baby brother, Danny. The damage was severe to the 6 story building, and we were told one woman had died.

My Mom and Dad never talked about it. At that very moment, we were homeless. My grandmother had an apartment where we were able to live for a short time. I remember going up dark curved stairs on 50 Carmine Street. We then moved to 74 ½ Carmine Street where I lived until I was 17 years old. It was a railroad apartment. You first entered a large kitchen area with a bathtub. To the right was the dining room which led to the living room. To the left of the kitchen was my Dad's new workspace, which led to a small bathroom. There was another door on the other side of the bathroom. As you entered this door, there was another apartment exactly like the one described. We also rented this apartment, but used the rooms for our bedrooms. We paid about $14 a month, per apartment. These were cold flat apartments with no heat or hot water. We had to supply the stoves and the coal to heat the apartment. We had a large coal stove in the kitchen which we used to keep warm and to cook with. We had to start the fires and also had two stoves in the bedrooms. My poor mom had to start the fires and keep them going during the day and throughout the night. Everyday someone would have to bring up pails of coal and wood, which was usually me, because my brothers seemed to disappear right around that time.

Reality:

One day reality set in as I was looking into the apartments across Carmine Street. I saw people wearing only T-Shirts in the middle of the winter in their homes. In my apartment, it was cold, and we had to wear sweaters and coats when we were inside. They called it "steam heat." Then I came to the realization that we were poor. Winter mornings were especially challenging when it was time to get dressed for school. In would come the clothes off the clothesline .... Frozen. We would have to thaw them out around the stove. Many times we would go to school with damp clothes on that would dry by lunchtime. As you can imagine, walking to school with damp clothes, wasn't exactly pleasant.

After my Dad lost his business, he had to take a night job with Bethlehem Steel as a coppersmith fitting pipes together on ships. One was called the *United States*. Since he no longer had a shop, he would get work from his old customers. He would often go into their homes and reupholster their furniture. He was a diabetic, and there was always a possibility that he could pass out from low blood sugar. My mom would send me on house calls with him. She would say, "In this pocket is sugar, stick that in his mouth, and the other pocket is smelling salts. Take the cap off and hold that under his nose." So I always went with him, one hand on the sugar, one on the smelling salts. I never had to use it, and that was okay with me, but it made me feel good that I could take care of him if he needed me.

At six years old, I realized, because my family was so poor, that I would never have much in my life. I said to myself, mom and dad would not have to take care of me, but I will take care of them. I began my quest for money. I saw a man shining shoes. He carried his business on his shoulder. I thought I could shine shoes. So, I found some scrap wood and built a shoe shine box. All I needed now was the polish rags and cleaner, it would cost about $2. So I collected 100 bottles with a 2 cents deposit. I had my $2 and went into business. I made my way to 8th Street and 6th Avenue, a very busy intersection, but made very little money. I guess people thought I might not be capable of giving them a good shoe shine. I didn't give up. I picked up another job. On Friday and Saturday nights, I would sell copies of the Daily News. At 8pm the paper would arrive at the newsstand on 8th Street. I would buy 20 newspapers for a nickel a piece and sell them for a dime, making a dollar profit. Sometimes, I would go out for a second run, making another dollar. Some people were really nice and would give me an extra nickel or dime. I would go into all the restaurants and bars up and down 8th Street. One time I was in a bar and a man shouted, "What are you doing kid?" I said, "I'm selling the Daily News." He replied, "Give me one." He reached for his wallet on the top of the bar table, and took out a bill and said, "Keep the change." It was a $10 dollar bill. I was numb all night. I never had so much money in all my life. In reality, I never had much at all. I never even had a birthday party or thought I ever would. Now, having some money, I decided to give myself a birthday party. My seventh birthday was coming up, and I invited all my friends to come over after school. I bought an assortment of candy and put them in dishes around the house. I remember it was Wednesday, specifically, Ash Wednesday. We were all Catholic and had ashes on our foreheads. It suddenly dawned on me. I had given up candy for Lent. I was the only one who didn't enjoy my birthday party!

 Having little money enabled me and my friends to get creative with ways to have fun. We often played kick the can on the four corners of Bedford and Downing Streets. It was a game similar to baseball. Home plate was where you kicked the can. If the other team caught the can in the air you would be out. If it landed on the ground you ran the bases. All you needed to play was 3-4 people on each team and an old can. Another game was stickball. All you needed for this game was an old broom stick and a Spalding rubber ball that cost 25 cents. If you didn't have the quarter, you could fish out a four foot long piece of wire from the sewer, roll it up into a ball and you were ready to play. Not having money didn't mean we couldn't have fun.

 My friends and I couldn't afford bikes so we decided to make our own scooters to get around. All you needed was an old skate, a 2X4 about 36" long, a few nails and a wooden apple or orange crate. We would walk down to the Bleecker Street market to pick out our crates, then down to the factories to get some scrap wood that was lying around. To make the scooter you would take the skate apart and nail it to both ends of the 2X4. Then you would nail the crate to the beam. You could also make a compartment to store stuff in with excess scrap wood. The final piece was attaching the handle bars. This was accomplished by nailing two pieces of wood to the top of the crate. Some kids adorned the front of their scooters with bottle caps. There you have it. Priceless transportation.

In the evening, if we didn't feel like taking a ride on our scooters, we would walk to Washington Square Park to play War, mostly just me, and my best friend Guy Parody. We made wooden guns, and found dirt balls, pretending they were grenades, and threw them. One particular evening we noticed something different when we looked across the street from the park. We went over to explore and detected a huge hole, the block had been completely demolished. We didn't know what to think of it, so we continued to play. There were so many dirt balls, which we were happy about, it meant more grenades for us to play with. We threw them down into the hole watching them explode. Little did we know, we were bombing the beginnings of what would become, New York University.

When we weren't busy playing War or Kick the Can, one of our favorite pastimes occurred on summer afternoons around 3 pm. A few of us would meet on Downing Street and wait for the bookies and loan sharks to come out of the bar. The ball game would be over. About 8 men would walk about 20 feet down the street and start a Craps game. The money would be dropped on the ground and transferred to the winner as the dice rolled. We would start praying, "God, please let the police come." After a while a patrol car would show up cruising the neighborhood. It came down Bedford and turned into Downing Street. As the police approached, all bets would cease, and whoever had the dice made sure they weren't on the ground. The money would be left and the gamblers nonchalantly walked away, separating into buildings and alleyways. The police would roll slowly down the street passing the scene. They never wanted to catch anyone, they just wanted to make a statement. Once the police passed, the money was ours. Sometimes there would be $20, $30 and even $40 dollars on the ground. We would split up the money, buy food or candy, then go to the movies. Each week we would pray for another Craps game. If we ran out of luck with the gamblers, I would resort to other measures to get some cash. On Carmine Street there were two stores. One was a trucking company called PM Transfer, and the other was a pet shop that sold mostly pigeons, and pigeon feed. Occasionally, they sold puppies or kittens. In the front of the store tied up to a post were about 10-20 bamboo poles. For 50 cents, I bought a pole and some bubble gum to stick on the tip. I became a coin collector. I would walk up 6th Avenue, look down the air shafts of the grates over the subways, where people often dropped their spare change. The money would land on a cement floor about 4 feet down. I would fish out the money for 100% profit.

As time went on, I was hired for my first job at age 9. Across the street from where I lived, was a Texaco gas station with a new owner. His name was Luke. When school started he asked me to pick up something for him at a butcher shop about a mile up 7th Avenue. By now, I had my own bike, and went and came back and earned a quarter. I did this a few times for him. Then he asked if I wanted to work after school at the gas station. I agreed and was excited to have a steady job. I would work every day from 3:30 – 6:00, and all day Saturday. I would earn $3.50/week and worked for him for 10 years. My first job was gassing up cars and trucks on that busy 7th Avenue location. I also would check the oil, battery, radiator level under the hood, and clean the windows on every car. I would come out and stand on a box so I could see under the hood. My pay wasn't the greatest but I made a lot of tips. By the time I was 10, I was driving cars on the lot. I also learned how to do quick lubes and oil changes, winterizing and summarizing cars. At 11 years old, I was driving cars onto the ramp, doing tune-ups, and shortly after, I began to do break jobs. I was always looking to make extra money.

In between gas ups, I wiped down cars every day for people who worked in the factories, cleaning the dust and soot off. I charged them $2 a week. That came to an extra $40 - $50 dollars a month. I was still only making $3.50 a week, so I had to find other ways to increase my income. A friend asked me if I knew anyone who would like to buy his truck. He would sell it for $75. The next day a neighbor told me his truck blew up and he needed to replace it. I told him to meet the next day at 6:30 pm at the gas station. That morning I checked out my friend's truck and bought it for $75. That night I sold it for $150. I made $75 in just a few hours. I was always looking for opportunities to make extra money, and had many.

I'm now 12 years old, and I took myself on a shopping spree. I had saved $2,000. I bought a horse. My friends and I would go horseback riding every Sunday for two hours, costing $16 a week, in Forest Hills, Queens. After more than a year of this, I figured out that if I bought a horse it would cost me $60/month to room board and maintain the animal in a box stall. So I bought a horse and could ride anytime I wanted. My parents, for the 8 room apartment, rent adjusted, were still paying $30/month. I was paying $60 for a horse. I also bought a new bike, some new clothes, a car and a new tape recorder. This is when I heard myself sing for the first time. As for the car, my dear older brother, Frankie, came to me with an offer. He said, "I have the license, you buy the car, and I'll drive you wherever you want to go." I agreed this was a good plan. Later on in life, I asked him how he had a license at 15 years old, and where did he get the registration? He said, "I made a cardboard plate, put it on the car, and never got stopped."

In that same year, I was still working at Luke's gas station when a particularly significant thing happened. Traffic cops would hang out in the back room of the gas station to write their summonses for the day, sometimes 2-3 in the station at a time. One day, three of them were having a heated discussion on what was considered a double-action firing, where two bullets could be discharged in a split second.

Two of the policemen left, but one of them, Policeman Daniels, had just been cleaning his gun and was now reassembling it. I was at the cash register about two feet from where he was sitting. The only thing separating us was an 18" divider. I could see him from where I was standing. He continued to muse about the double firing. I heard him say "This is a double-action!" The gun was pointed at me, and he did not realize it was loaded, when it went off the bullet flew passed me, about one inch from my head. It hit the clock, went through the wall, cracking a brick in a building across 7th Avenue. The two of us were frozen numb to think of what could have transpired. Somehow, by the grace of God, the gun was pointed slightly upward, just enough to miss hitting me. Policeman Daniels was shaking like a leaf! He quit the force within 6 months and never came back to the gas station. I saw him one more time before retiring. He was a wreck and talking to himself. I just went on with my life, always in survival mode. Besides, I still wanted to enjoy all the things I had bought for myself. Twelve was quite a year. I went on a huge shopping spree. Jackie Gleason asked me to sing for him and I almost got shot in the head. Wow, what a year.

Summer Time:

· Summer came, and I went to the Greenwich House Summer Camp for the second year. I loved it so much I didn't want to come home. I always cried when I had to come back to the heat infested city, with brick and cement everywhere that held the heat of the day, all through the night, like a brick oven. The relief was across the street. The Leroy Street Pool. Just on an angle from my apartment was a park where you played softball which also had an indoor and outdoor swimming pool, perfect for the hot summer days. It cost about 10 cents and you could stay all day, or until you were hungry. For a quarter, you could get a bologna sandwich on French bread at the deli on Carmine Street, and a Pepsi for another dime. I could hear my stomach growl as the food went down.

One day I was all by myself at the pool. I swam for a while, then got out of the water, to warm up in the sun. I saw a mosquito land on my arm. It was looking for a good spot to bite me. I watched it probing around. Suddenly I had this thought, and I said, *"God you made this mosquito, and you can make him not bite me."* The mosquito, after resting some more, flew off without biting me. The most peculiar thing is that all summer long when a mosquito landed on me it would always fly away without a bite. I think it made me believe God was real. The next summer, the first mosquito that landed on my arm bit me. Okay, now that I know God is real, so are mosquitos. That event affected me my whole life. Later on, when I was in my twenties, I was about to wash my car at a friend's house in Staten Island. There was a problem. The water spigot outside was infested with busy bees, going in and out of the small opening all around the spigot. I had to hook the hose up and turn the water on to wash my car. Do I dare do this and upset the bees? I thought back to the mosquito. I said, *"God, you made these bees and you can make them not sting me"*. I found a little courage. I slowly hooked up the hose, bees swirling around my hand. I slowly turned on the water, washed my car, and slowly turned the water off, disconnecting the hose. God did more for me than just not getting a bee sting.

Being a songwriter, I often tried to interpret the world around me. I started thinking more about God, and in my songs I started to ask questions. Was there really a man called Abraham? Is there really a town called Bethlehem? As time went on, I forgot about the mosquitos and bees. Another incident brought those memories back in full force. I was a bit older now, and I was out with two of my sons, John Eugene and Mark. We were at a campsite in Tennessee. I explained to them what the boundaries were by pointing out a large tree on one side of the site and several other markers on the other. It wasn't too long after that I heard a scream. I ran towards the kids and saw John Eugene on the other side of a large tree standing on an active beehive. There were hundreds of bees flying all around him. They were inside his shirt and pants and all over his body. I ran over and carefully removed him from the hive. I took his clothes off realizing he had not one sting. The only thing I could say was,

"Thank you God." These memories became embedded in my mind and heart.

The Singer Emerges:

    I don't remember when I started singing. My family told me I was around 3 years old. I used to wind up my grandmother's Victrola to play her records. I was told that I would sing the songs and cry with tears in my eyes, always hitting the high notes with deep emotion as I Sang "Pagliacci" along with the Great Caruso.

    I began to sing at family functions and my mom would play the accordion. I remember, each time I had to use the restroom at school, I had to pass by Mrs. Cavecchio's room. She would stop me in the hall and wouldn't let me go until I sang a song for her whole class. I was never embarrassed to sing in front of all the students. I felt proud that I could make people happy by singing popular songs on the radio. Mrs. Cavecchio was also proud and pleased to have me sing for her class.

    Mrs. Cavecchio wasn't the only one who enjoyed hearing me sing. When I was 9 years old, everything changed in my life. It started in the summer when a man named Joey, from the PM Trucking Company on Carmine Street, asked me to come with him on his truck route. It was so much fun. We would go to locations in uptown NYC. I would jump on the back of the truck, and at various stops, would push off these lightweight bundles. Maybe 10-20 packages per stop. All along the way, Joey would be playing drum beats on his steering wheel to songs on the radio, and I would sing. Every now and then, at the end of the week, Joey would take me to the back of the trucking store where 10 or more drivers would congregate after receiving their pay. Joey would announce, OK. Everybody, the kid is gonna sing a couple of songs." When I was done singing, Joey would pass a hat around and would give me the money the truckers put in it. There would be $20 or more dollars in the hat.

    One Friday evening, when I was about 12 years old, Luke asked me to go to the French restaurant across the street and pick up a dinner he had called in for. I walked in with my green Texaco outfit with the little red star on my shirt. The owner, Paul, came up to me and said, excitedly, "Jackie Gleason wants you to sing for him!" I looked up, and in front of me, Jackie was sitting with two beautiful show girls, with a drink in his hand. He very loudly said, "Sing Kid." My heart sank. I thought of my mom and dad. My dad was sick and my mom wasn't well. I thought he would take me away from my family who needed me. I put my head down and walked out. Sometimes kids do things for reasons they don't understand, but I knew exactly what I was doing.

Two years after meeting Jackie Gleason, I was about to experience a big change. It was my last year at P. S. 3, the school only went to the 9th grade. On my 14th birthday, I was home from school, perhaps sick, and I found a 45 rpm record my younger sister Mary had bought. It was a fairly new recording by Frankie Lymon & the Teenagers. I had never heard the song before, I played it and loved it. It was called "Why do Fools Fall in Love?" I learned the song, and found enjoyment in the happy, upbeat tunes of Doo-Wop music. Finally, I found something inspiring which added lightness to my life. This was short lived. About two weeks after a tragic thing happened. My Dad passed away. It was a hard time for our family, however, we managed to get through the summer. In September, I would be going to Murray Hill Vocational High School. It was the oldest building I had seen in my life. It ended up being condemned and we were placed in Brooklyn Automotive H.S. the next year. This school was mostly populated by Blacks and Hispanics. One day, I went to the bathroom. There were three guys harmonizing by the sinks. I went into a stall. They started to sing background vocals to that song I loved so much, "Why do Fools Fall in Love?" No one was singing the lead. All of a sudden, out of my mouth, in perfect timing to their background, came the words: *"Why do birds sing so gay? And lovers await the break of day? Why do they fall in love?"* I sang to the end of the song. I stepped out of the stall and we were all amazed at the perfect blend of our voices. One spoke, his name was Victor Crespo. He stuttered some, but not when he sang. He said, "Do you want to start a club? He meant a singing group. Within a few short months, we recorded our first record called, *"You I Adore."* The flip side was *"It's Over Now."* The Young Tones had begun. I'll stop here. My life is just one of the many lives coming out of Greenwich Village.

• • • • • • • • ● ○○○○○○ ○ ○ ○

Charles Messina

The Bomber Boys

The Bomber Boys were cool. I wanted to be a Bomber Boy. I could never be a Bomber Boy. I wasn't old enough. I wasn't tough enough. I didn't even own a Bomber.

The Bomber Boys were a group – a gang – an assemblage – of teenage kids from the South Village neighborhood of my youth in the early 1980's. They were what every teenage boy who saw *"The Outsiders"* wanted to be. Except this was a few years before that film was released. Talk about being ahead of your time!

Actually, young men in black leather jackets trying to act cool is about as old as black leather jackets themselves. When you throw in a popped up fur collar, well, then you have a Bomber. Add a teenager with a chip on his shoulder, and there you have a Bomber Boy. But before the Bomber Boys made strutting across Bleecker Street in black leather attire fearsome, there were other leather clad young men who donned the cowhide in the name of eternal coolness. Brando in *"The Wild One"* was the iconic bad boy in his biker jacket (with the hat to match.) Travolta in *"Grease"* flew the flag with his T Birds gang insignia emblazoned on the back. And then there was Fonzie, who just might have been the original Bomber Boy. A man so tough, so filled with libidinal energy, he could punch a jukebox and make it play his favorite song. The ladies swooned. Aaayyy!

Black leather can have an effect on people. Those putting it on and those taking it in. There was no shortage of it to spot on the streets of Greenwich Village in the 80's, that's for sure. Any number of shops along Christopher Street had various fetish items for sale: chaps, caps, jockstraps – for a different crowd perhaps. But black leather apparel in the Village was not a new thing. However, in life, as in fashion, it often happens that everything old is new again. The Bomber Boys had a different goal in mind: they brought black leather jackets back but with a twist – their brand was Italian American street swagger.

A jacket doesn't make you tough. A jacket doesn't make you cool. A jacket can make you *look* tough and cool. Like the fedora before it, it was a symbol. A gangster in a fedora is a gangster out of a fedora. The fedora is the cherry on top. The Bomber Boys were tough kids before they started wearing jackets. The jackets just sent the message out, loud and clear, don't mess with any guy wearing one, or else your messing with *every* guy wearing one. The basic principle of Gangs 101.

The South Village of the 1980's was still trying to hold onto its tribal ways. The Italian American enclave, which it had been since the turn of the century, was fraying at the edges. A step up in class had some Italians trading in the brick and mortar of tenements for porches of grass in the suburbs. It was considered upward mobility in society. Progress. A sign of shedding the shackles of poverty for a place in the sun, in Staten Island or New Jersey. Very few of the locals could have predicted that those two-room walk up apartments they inhabited in roach infested buildings would become *chic* and subsequently soar in value. It was unfathomable to the old timers that the very places they were eager to escape would be so desirable for so many to get into. But that is exactly what happened. The rent controlled rooms that were going for $100 a month, would eventually cost $1,000, $2,000, $3,000 and more. It was all about location, location, location. The Village was coveted in large part because of the community built there by Italian Americans who kept it clean and safe for decades. Sure, you had the art world, the gay community and NYU. But the heart of the Village for hundreds of years before that was the Italians who settled there, and raised their children there. They took pride in the neighborhood. They made it their home. They made it a place that others would also want to call home.

At any one time, in any one building, you could find three generations of a family living under the same roof. Grandma on the third floor. Daughter on the second floor and granddaughter on the ground floor. If you checked the names on the doorbells, they would all have ended in vowels. Religion was also a big part of life in the neighborhood. Three churches in the Village formed the Bermuda Triangle of Catholicism. There was St. Anthony's on Sullivan, Our Lady of Pompeii on Carmine and St. Joseph's on 6th Avenue. All those churches within a ¼ mile of each other meant that forgiveness was never more than a few blocks away. For those who needed it.

The Village has always been a conglomerate of different people. Different values. Different styles. In the 1980's, outside influences, or what would later be called gentrification, started to encroach more and more upon Tribal sacred ground. Thompson Park had yuppies in it, transvestites (who worked in local bars) started moving into buildings, designers were renting storefronts. But the natives were hanging on. The giant Italian flag was still painted on the wall of the handball court. Even though some were getting restless. There were those who just didn't like different, who wanted to keep the status quo. Change was just too scary. They were proprietary and wanted to show ownership. They wanted to make it clear whose neighborhood it had been and whose it still was. What better way to exemplify uniformity than with everyone wearing the same uniform. Like, say, a black leather bomber jacket.

It seems to have started on a lark. One kid in the neighborhood thought it would be a cool idea if he and some of his friends wore a bomber jacket. It was probably inspired more by popular gang movies such as *"The Warriors,"* and *"The Wanderers,"* than by real life gangs like The Hells Angels or the Latin Kings These were teenage kids trying to project an image. Trying to stand out during a pretty crowded time for authenticity. There were a lot of firsts during this time period. Vibrant forms of expression in art, music, and dress, were happening everywhere. Hip Hop was new. There was punk rock too. And Breakdancing. Preppies. The Brat Pack. Valley Girls. Power suits on Wall Street. Everybody had a costume. A guy named Michael Jackson would soon put on a red leather jacket and a glove to intercede and "Beat" gang violence. It was all happening at once. So, while a group of teenagers wearing black leather wasn't revolutionary, it was distinctive enough. It was a streetwise fashion statement.

Gang activity in New York City goes back centuries. There is a long tradition of ethnic conflict among the impoverished. Poor people have nothing. So they protect whatever they perceive to be theirs. Even if there so- called turf is nothing more than a street corner. The city was awash in gangs in the early 1980's, a leftover from the bloodbath of the 1970's, with most of the activity confined to areas such as Harlem or the Bronx. The various uniforms they wore were a way for the members to brandish their loyalty and intimidate their rivals in the process. While the initial intent of a gang is often to form a brotherhood, the result is almost always violence and crime.

In the 1980's, before the internet or social media, something went "viral" through word of mouth. That's how people found out about something. Street gangs got their reputations through their actions and by spreading fear through threats of attack. One gang in this era who marketed this type of psychological panic throughout the city were The Deceptions. Named after the shape shifting *Transformers* from the television cartoon, they intimidated, jumped and robbed innocent high schoolers across the city. While they were known to travel in packs and overwhelm single victims on their way home from school, or on trains, perhaps their biggest influence was the psychological terror they imposed. They didn't wear any uniforms, so you couldn't easily identify them. Like a good Deception, they blended in. They could be anybody. Quite an ingenious and horrifying approach to deceive their prey and elude law enforcement. A typical Deception offensive went this way: Someone would sound the alarm about them and word would spread that the Deceptions were coming, and that meant they'd be waiting for you outside your school. Fear of the unknown was the greatest weapon of the Deceptions. You could imagine a gang of hundreds out there, armed with box cutters and hammers and ready to pounce. The reality was, city wide, they were probably about 60 or so, truly dedicated members, of the gang in all. But they could expand to hundreds when necessary through local off shoot gangs such as the LoLifes or the RicoCons.

I can remember when the rumor spread through my all-boys Catholic High School in Manhattan. Someone got wind of – or made up – the idea that the Deceptions were going to be outside at dismissal. It led to many kids going home early for fear that it was true. Others vowed to band together and fight them if necessary – with the football team, if possible! The headmaster called the police. The Deceptions never showed up that afternoon. But the thought that they might at any point lasted forever. That's street warfare of the highest caliber.

At a time when Deceptions roamed the Earth, what could a band of mostly Italian American kids from the Village do to protect themselves and their neighborhood? Form a gang of their own, of course. Well, maybe it wasn't in direct response to any threat, or to any threat at all, but it just seemed like the right thing to do. So one kid tells another kid this idea about wearing bomber jackets. It catches on. Soon, a few more are doing it. And a few more. By now, a bunch of them are wearing these jackets, parading around the neighborhood and calling themselves The Bomber Boys. That's how you start a gang.

Once the name and the uniform are in place, a gang needs turf, a place to hang out and claim as their own. The Bomber Boys were a pretty transient bunch. I recall them being on the move a lot. Walking. Stalking. Hawking. In groups of three or four. Sometimes I'd see them sitting on park benches, huddled around a radio. Smoking. Drinking. They seemed to always be out in the street. That takes a stunning dedication to idle time. No hobbies. No sports. No schoolwork. Just preening and posing. A complete commitment to the perception of being a hoodlum is a full time job. Some came from troubled backgrounds and broken homes, but others did not. Their communality was that they were joined together by the brotherhood of the jacket. And a devotion to mischief.

The South Village had long been a territory governed by its own rules. The laws of the street. The way of the Mafia. Doctors and lawyers were fine. Accountants and teachers, eh. The thing to aspire to, for impressionable young Italian American men, growing up in the Village of this era, was to become a mobster. Several generations of men were reared on the lie of the street reputation. That there was honor in organized crime. That crime pays. What starts as childhood pranks and misbehavior can quickly spiral into vandalism and violence. Loitering can lead to looting. Purposelessness can lead you to prison. A search for respect can take you down the wrong path right into a dead end. With a patch of scorched earth left behind you. Teenagers with too much time on their hands usually get themselves into trouble. Trouble is the gateway to crime. The Bomber Boys set homeless people on fire. They punched people in the face for looking at their girlfriends. They drop kicked gay couples walking through their territory.

What started out as an attempt to bond, or be cool or protect the neighborhood, quickly devolved into a menacing situation. This notion of protection is one that went back centuries. The roots extend to Sicilian gangs, formed to protect themselves against invaders. These gangs created their own system of justice. They would eventually begin to extort money from local landowners in exchange for protection. This system was brought to America by Sicilians and Southern Italians who immigrated here, into communities like the South Village. Honored as tradition by locals for many years, it turned into a racket. The defenders became the destroyers. Instead of being guardians, they became bullies. Being tough doesn't mean picking on the weak, or the helpless, or taking advantage of your own. But gang mentality can influence people to do stupid things. I knew some of The Bomber Boys pretty well. I played whiffle ball with them growing up. I admired some of them. I sure liked their jackets. But too much time on the street and the wrong influences will turn anybody bad. Fights, alcohol, drugs and gangster aspirations will wreck even the nicest kids. It'll turn them. Some of the Boys went down a really bad road that led to addiction, or prison. A few did both. One died.

It's remarkable the things that you're taken with when you're a kid. The people that influence you and what they seem like from afar. Like a car mirror. From a distance objects in the mirror appear much cooler than they are. Once you see them up close, the truth is revealed. Beneath it all, there's an insecurity, an uncertainty, a fear. Even in the toughest tough guy. Even in Fonzie, I bet. Because tough is a façade. It's used to hide vulnerability. Black leather is good protection against exposure. It's thick and durable. But it's not bulletproof. Sooner or later it gets penetrated. I was talking to a former Bomber Boy some years ago and he told me that another kid in the gang who attended a public school would never wear his bomber jacket to school. I asked, Why not? He said he was afraid he would get his ass kicked! There's always somebody tougher.

When I was a student at NYU looking for an internship in the film and television industry, I landed an interview with a production company shooting in NYC at the time. It was the Second Assistant Director's job to meet with the prospective interns like myself. Admittedly, not an enviable gig. I met with this person in a very informal manner – standing in a hallway in a makeshift production office in SoHo and chatting for a few minutes. It was a cold day, and I remember I wore a leather jacket, I had bought in a Banana Republic store. It wasn't black. It was brown and didn't have a fur collar. It had a flat one. In the middle of a very innocuous conversation, this Second Assistant Director stopped and looked at me. He asked me, "What's with the leather jacket?" I looked at him incredulously, and replied, "What do you mean?" He repeated, "The leather jacket. Are you a tough guy or something?" I was stunned. For half a second I was flattered. Then I was insulted. The question was so out of place and out of line that I don't even remember my reply. I think it was something along the lines of "This jacket? It isn't even mine." I felt like a moron. I was also confused. This guy's perception of a leather jacket, *any* leather jacket, and anyone in one, was that the wearer must be a tough guy? A part of me had always wished it was that easy. Now I was embarrassed, for myself, and for the poor cow who gave up his skin for this mortifying moment. I didn't get the internship. I didn't want it after that exchange. I wish I could remember that guy's name. I've googled the film he was working on at the time. Nothing looked familiar. Still, to this day, the incident annoys me so much that if I could find that Second Assistant Director, I would reach out to him. I would meet with him under the guise of talking about something business related, and, in true Bomber Boys fashion, I would punch him in the face.

• • • • • • • • ● ○ ○ ○ ○ ○ ○ ○ ○ ○ ○

Frederick (Freddy Bop) Nocetti

I Wouldn't Change A Thing

Here I am in the center of the capital of the world – born and raised on 6th Avenue and Bleecker Street, actually Carmine Street, facing Father Demo Square.

My family owned the building and hardware store "Nocetti Hardware," Golden Pizza was on the corner – later to become Joe's Pizza – Bob Dylan lived on my block and Jimi Hendrix lived around the corner on Bedford Street. It was the best neighborhood – gangsters, freaks, and fairies and a whole lot of Italians. It was our neighborhood but there were always outsiders coming into the area, day and night. I thought that everyone lived like this. Why go anywhere else. There was music, girls, bars and coffee houses.

In the winter, we'd be having snowball fights in Washington Square Park, 4th Street Park to us. After almost freezing, we would go to the Café Wha? And for 25 cents we could warm up. Once we saw Jimi Hendrix perform there for a quarter!

I always had fights in the neighborhood. For some reason guys always wanted to fight with me. It was about the GIRLS. They liked me, so the guys wanted to fight me. Sometimes I won, sometimes I lost. Either way, I still got the girl. Neighborhood ladies would yell at me to stop fighting or they would tell my mother. I'd say, "You don't know my mother Mona", and they would reply, "Your mother is Rita." I'd get home and for sure my mother heard about the fights and would beat me with a wooden spoon. The same spoon she would use to stir the gravy. She would break it over my head, then send me downstairs to my grandfather's store to get another one.

When my son was born, my father told me, "Don't hit your kids, let your wife hit them, you're too strong." It was great advice dad! Then I realized that he never hit me. He would grab me by the neck, pull me against the wall, cock his arm and say, "Do you understand." I'd say yes, and that would be the end of it. Then my mother would start the beating. It's great going back, remembering those days. I wouldn't change a thing.

We had the best music, cars and no cell phones. Yeah, I'd do it again and I wouldn't change none of it.

Another Neighborhood Story

It was 1970, I was 18, me, and a few of my friends were having a slice in Golden Pizza. Some younger guys from the neighborhood and some guys we knew from Bleecker Street were already there. We all knew who we were, all from the neighborhood. We knew each other.

Then, three guys come in and started up with the younger kids. With that, the kids left, and the 3 "outsiders" followed them out. We all got up, that was it. When something like that happened, one of us would whistle, "Pop Goes the Weasel," and when you got to the word "Pop," it's on! Night sticks for them.

One of the three guys started beating up on the guys from Bleecker Street, so I grabbed him, and started to whale on him. This was all happening right in front of my family's building (11 Carmine Street,) and all of a sudden, I could hear the windows opening and my mother and other neighbors in the building yelling, "You *non illegitimi*, stop fighting or I'll call the cops. Then the sound of sirens and ambulances. Everyone splits and the guys from Bleecker Street are thanking me for helping them. About an hour later, I went home. I opened the door. My shirt is ripped and blood stained. My mother is yelling, "You were in that fight." I said yes ma, and you called the cops on me.

The next day we went to Carmine Street gym and the guys from the other end of Bleecker Street were there. We joked about the whole thing. Then we started to hang out together. About this time, I knew some older guys who had a club (it used to be a store) that was now a neighborhood hangout for cool guys. It was located on Bedford Street. The members were getting an apartment and giving up the club. They offered it to me and my friends. That's how it worked in the neighborhood. For generations these clubs would be handed down from the older guys to the younger ones. So, now we had a club!

The rent was $100 a month. There were 20 of us so it cost $5 a head. We had a jukebox and would have parties on Friday nights. We sold drinks for 50 cents. The rent was always paid on time. The club was great, we always had someplace to go. A place where all the guys and girls could hang out.

Then my sister, Carol, married and moved to Spring Street. Her apartment was payed for by the "Wise" guys. They paid the rent, electricity and phone. They took numbers there (bets on horse races) and used the phone for three hours each day from 12-3 pm. That was the arrangement. My sister's husband wasn't going to live there anymore and offered the apartment to me. It was much better than the club on Bedford, which was getting too crowded. Twenty people was too much!

That summer in 1970, I went to Europe for 2 months. My buddy Frankie Dee stayed in the apartment. He would put his amp in front of the window and play his guitar. He would practice for hours, particularly the song, "Four Day Creep," by the group Humble Pie. He would play it over and over. By the time I returned, the landlord was ready to evict me from the apartment. Anyway, I smoothed things over with him and told him who my family was, and he let me stay.

One day I'm watching late night TV. Peter Frampton was on and talking about a summer he spent in SoHo. He had rented an apartment in what he thought was going to be a quiet place. It turned out that in the building he was renting an apartment in, there was this crazy guy trying to play his song, Four Day Creep, all summer long!

• • • • • • • • ●○○○○○○○ ○ ○

David Noferi

Leroy Street Pool

I remember a night when we all got together. What a great crew! We met at Leroy Street Pool. It was me, the Shark (Dennis Guglielmo), Butch (Al Canecchia), Dennis Genovese and the pool's lifeguard, Bob Daly. Ziggy (Bobby Andriani) and Richie Palandrani, also a lifeguard, were probably there too. It was the night of the great NYC "blackout," November, 9th, 1965. We shined flashlights into the pool. Butch and Dennis were singing. If Ziggy was there, he was harmonizing too, and perhaps strumming a guitar? We only had the flashlights and the full moon as a light source, WOW!

All of these friends I hold very close to my heart. That's when "neighborhood was neighborhood." We had a great time that night. After all of the fun, I went into the streets with my flashlight to help neighbors see while crossing the streets. I also helped out some drivers by giving directions. This was just one night of the many great times I've had growing up in the Village.

Richie Havens, Tony Orlando And Me

Let me preface these stories by saying I have an uncanny resemblance to the singer and celebrity, Tony Orlando, who became popular in American culture during the 1970's.

One day my wife Toni and I, went down to the Museum of the American Indian for a nice day out together. When we entered the building, a Hispanic man, the curator, stopped us dead in our tracks. He was so excited stating, "You're Tony Orlando, Oh my God. I can't believe it. I think you're great!"

He went on and on. He took a dollar bill out of his wallet and asked me to autograph it. Never did I refuse to write one. I realized early on, that it was easier to go along than to convince these people that I was not who they thought me to be. I signed Tony Orlando on that dollar bill. He couldn't believe it. He said, "I'm going to frame this bill when I get home."

My wife whispered to me, "If he finds out the truth, you're going to get framed for impersonating Tony Orlando!" Then the curator started to speak in Spanish. The real Tony Orlando is Puerto Rican and Greek. I, of course, am of Italian ancestry. I figured this is where they got me? My wife, adroitly steps in and answers the curator in fluent Spanish, saying, "Tony has a sore throat, so I will speak for him." After a few words we went into the museum.

About eight years ago, my wife Toni and I went to Yankee Stadium to see the Bombers play. While seated before the game started, my wife heard her name Toni being called out. She looked around to see who may have known her? To no avail, she could not recognize anyone. She decided to stand up and look around. To her amazement, all the onlookers were pointing at me, "Yes Tony, they said to her, Tony Orlando."

My wife sat down and said, "David, here we go again. They think you are Tony Orlando." It was the week of the Jerry Lewis Muscular

Dystrophy Telethon. So, I stood up and waved to the crowd. I told them. "Remember Jerry's kids and don't forget to donate money this weekend."

When I sat down my wife, the real Toni, started to laugh. Reason being that if I were the real Tony Orlando why would I be sitting in the Bleachers? The cheap seats. I should be sitting in a box seat. They must be saying what a skin flint Tony Orlando must be!

There were many adventures as Tony Orlando, especially when I would hang out with Richie Havens. I met him in the Village early on in his career and we became friends. One time, I was on the house boat that Richie kept at the 72nd Street Boat Basin. He owned a thirty foot boat called, "The Lazarus." We would go fishing in that boat.

John Fischer, a chauffeur, who drove John Lennon's white psychedelic Rolls Royce, became a friend and would sometimes join us on these fishing ventures. One day we were all sitting on the houseboat, when a guy from the music business, who happened to be a guest on the boat, kept staring at me. He finally approached and said, "Hey Tony Orlando, I did some pictures of you a few years ago, and I never got paid for them?" Both John and Richie looked at me. I don't know how they kept straight faces. I told the guy, "Take it up with my manager." So he grunted and walked away. Wow, that was a close one. We all couldn't stop laughing over this scene. We set the boat to sail and enjoyed the day out in the sun

Another time, Richie, Dennis P. (Richie's road manager) and I were all together. Dennis P. taught me how to run a sound board. We took a trip upstate to see a friend of Richie's, named Robert Thurman. He was the first American to be ordained as a Buddhist priest in the USA. He was a professor at Columbia University. Robert approached me and said, "Tony Orlando, it's so nice to meet you." As usual, I played along with it, I just couldn't resist. We were at his beautiful home and swam in his indoor pool. We went into his study room. We had a wonderful time. His young children were there as well. One of his daughters would grow up to be the actress, Uma Thurman.

Needless to say, my friend Richie Havens was a good man and a brother to me. I had an urn with my mother's father's and brother's ashes. I so wanted my family to go beyond the USA. Richie said, "No problem, give me the ashes," and so I did. He went on a beautiful vacation to the South of France. He gave me a video of this wonderful experience. Richie is on a boat, he lifts a glass of Champagne and says, "David, this one's for you and your family." He releases the ashes of my mother Muriel, my father Bobby Sr. and my brother Bobby Jr. into Lake Geneva, between Switzerland and France. This made me very happy.

I will always remember a day in July, 1969. Richie, who lived across the street from me on Downing Street, called me up in the early hours of the morning and invited me to watch the moon landing with him. We had a good buzz on. I love and miss Richie Havens, the man, and the friend. What a great guy!

Louis Nunez

Remembrances Of A Village Kid

Growing up in Greenwich Village in the 1950's and 1960's was a magical time, in retrospect. Of course, while doing so, we thought nothing of it. This was normal life. We lived two blocks south of Houston Street, right on 6th Avenue. My sister and I lived in a two and ½ room apartment that my parents had lived in since they had gotten married during WW II, and had not left, even while raising two children. My sister and I slept in the living room. While my sister, who was five years younger than I was, still slept in a crib in my parents' bedroom, my mother would put me to sleep on her side of the bed. When they were ready to sleep, she would open the Castro convertible bed and put me in it, so that I would awaken in the morning in our living room. Once my sister was big enough, she got the Castro bed and they bought a sofa bed that I slept in.

We lived in an Italian neighborhood. Most people didn't realize it back then, and to a certain extent also today, Manhattan's living neighborhoods were very ethnic. Uptown we had German town (the Yorktown area) and the lower East side was very Jewish. Downtown, below Delancey Street was considered Jewish town as well and I can remember walking with my father on Sundays down to that section of the city to buy stuff because at that time, they were the only stores open. They were, of course, closed on Saturdays.

I went to Our Lady of Pompeii grammar school on Bleecker

Street, just south of 6th Avenue. It was not yet referred to as the Avenue of the Americas. I went to pre-Kindergarten, Kindergarten and then up through the 8th grade. Unfortunately, in some ways, I had gotten sick while in Kindergarten with the mumps, measles and chicken pox, either together, or in sequence. My mother, who was a teacher, brought books for me to read while I was in bed, convalescing, so my reading level was quite good. Being the mother she was, she then pushed for me to be put into the first grade because I was bored in Kindergarten. Mother Superior said she would test me and gave me the first grade semester final exam to take. My mother objected, but Mother Superior won out. I took the tests (reading and math) and got 90's on both of them. (I still have those papers that my mother saved.) So, I was put into the first grade for the second semester.

Being the smallest boy in the class, I would often get into fights and come home dirty and with torn clothes. There were bullies in the class but we dealt with it. As a result, when my son was born, we held him back for a year so that he was one of the oldest in the class and not the youngest.

Spring and fall were times to play outside. We would play alley-ball in an alley between two buildings on Varick Street. Hitting 4 walls with the Spalding ball was considered a home run, if it wasn't caught, three walls a triple, and so on. Rocco Iacovone was one of my classmates who played with us.

Summer time was always wonderful. As a child, if it was really hot, someone in the neighborhood would secure a large wrench and open up a fire hydrant so that we would have our own local fountain to cool off in.

One day, my mother took me shopping with her to the butcher shop run by Phil and Jimmy, two WW II vets. I was outside the store and saw a red box with a handle on it and it said "pull." I didn't see the letters above the handle that said, "in case of fire." So, being ever inquisitive, I pulled it. Alarms started to go off and my mother came running out and grabbed me and pulled me inside the butcher store. We waited until the fire engines came and left. I never did that again!

We didn't have skate boards back then, but we improvised by taking an old metal roller skate and separating it so we had a front and back set of wheels that were then nailed to a 2X4. We then took an old vegetable crate and nailed that to the end of the wooden beam. Smaller pieces of wood arranged transversely across the top of the box provided the handlebars, and *voila*, we had our own little scooter for running around on.

We used to play in Washington Square Park. There was a big arch there, sort of a knock off of the *Arc d'Triompe* that stands in Paris. On the side of the arch was a small ledge that was perfect for hitting Spalding balls against. We used to play our version of baseball. We would hit the ball against the ledge and then run to first base. If you didn't hit the ledge just right, you would produce a ground ball that could easily be caught. If, on the other hand, you hit the ledge point on, the ball would fly into the air, and you could round the bases for a home run!

There was a park on Houston Street and 6th Avenue where we would play baseball and basketball. Sometimes, some of the local girls would come by and stand against the chain link fence and watch the boys play. Years later, when I had an orthopedic practice, Pete Seeger and his wife came in for consultation. We started talking about Greenwich Village and the people we knew. His wife, Toshi, looked at me while we were conversing and said, "I remember you playing ball in Houston Street Park." You could have blown me over with a feather!

We had the St. Anthony's feast on Thompson Street in the spring, our neighborhood's competition to the San Gennaro feast of Little Italy on Mulberry Street. They served, as I recall, the best sausage and pepper sandwiches and fried *Zeppole*.

After grammar school I attended St. Francis Xavier H.S. on 16th Street. We had bus passes and some of my classmates who had not gone to Pompeii would get on the bus with me. It was not a long ride, but we had book bags that were so heavy, we couldn't walk the mile or so, thus we rode on the bus.

One summer, after graduating high school, I was walking down

MacDougal Street. It was hot and being 18, I was able to have alcohol. I stopped and went into the Minetta Bar and ordered a beer. A gentleman was standing next to me and when I got the glass I turned to him to raise it, and Bob Dylan raised his back. I didn't bother him as I felt he deserved his privacy.

There are many other stories I could tell, but the one thing that is certain, is that there is no place else in the world to rival Greenwich Village. Paris may have Montmatre and London its Picadilly Square, but the Village is special in many ways. It was the home to many artists such as O'Henry, Poe, and Edna St Vincent Millay. So much history happened here. I feel blessed to have grown up in this part of the world!

Jean Paladino

The Village

Known to others who grew outside its boundaries of Houston Street to 14th Street, It's Greenwich Village. For us who grew up there it's, The Village, just as we say, The Bronx, we say The Village.

We always know when we meet someone from The Village because they know our nicknames and that's how we would still be addressed, no matter how long it's been since we lived there or have seen them.

We never knew how lucky we were to grow up there. More important, as a child, I never felt unlucky. It was a village where everything we needed was there. As they say it takes a village!

As a practicing psychotherapist, I know that growing up in a tenement building at 111 MacDougal Street, was probably the best therapy I ever had. I'm grateful to think back about the simple but what had to be complicated difficult times that we grew up in.

Many of our mothers raised us as only parents during our early years. Our fathers were away in World War II. They had so little but were able to make us feel as if we never had to do without.

Our mothers and grandmothers and aunts and women who were our neighbors worked in the factories in the garment district not far from the Village in what now would be lower Chelsea, probably around 23rd Street and 6th Avenue.

None of the mothers could ever afford to miss even a day of work.

I can remember, if one of us got sick with the measles, or whatever, we would all be put together so we could be sick at the same time. Then, only one of the adults would have to stay home from work to take care of all of us at the same time. How ingenious, the need to survive.

Thinking about it, the definition of family was so different for us then. Some of my fondest memories of family were sitting around my grandmother's kitchen table helping my mother and aunts with "piecework" they brought home from the factories to make some extra money. We lived on MacDougal Street on the corner of Minetta Lane, above the Minetta Tavern. Our rent then, was less than the hamburgers they now serve for $25 dollars.

Most of my mother's family lived across 6th Avenue on Carmine Street. Our apartments were extensions of one another's. My maternal grandmother lived on the third floor at 11 Carmine Street and had a bathtub. That was a big deal. That's where we would go to bathe. On MacDougal Street, we only had a toilet and in the kitchen, a wash tub where clothes would be washed by hand. I would sit on the cover of the wash tub and dangle my feet into the only sink in the apartment.

My mother's youngest sister lived with her family on the fourth floor in my grandmother's building and another older sister and her family on the fifth floor of that building. Doors were also open or at least unlocked. Privacy? Did we understand or did we ever seek privacy as something we would have wanted? Did we know what it was?

I now have to wonder and can feel very sad to think how difficult it had been for our parents. For all the adults in our lives. How did they do it? I now know how privileged I was to be an only child. I had a little more space, not having to share a room with a brother or sister. The rooms on MacDougal Street were probably smaller than what a small walk-in closet would be today. Apartments at 11 Carmine just a bit larger.

For a child, these extended families and extended homes gave us security and a place where we felt belonged. That was home.

The streets of the Village were as much our home as were our tiny apartments. The scale of the streets fostered a sense of security and feeling connected. I guess we would now say they gave us an "identity."

The not so tall buildings and the narrow streets like MacDougal, Sullivan and Thompson, gave us the ability to cross them in just a hop, skip and a jump. As kids we would traverse these streets without feeling any danger. Even crossing the vastness of 6th Avenue. I have no memory of any fear crossing "the Avenue." Of course, there were so few cars then. All the little parks that lined the Avenue were filled with people we knew. We also were cognizant that we were accountable to any of our neighbors, who could and would report back to our families, our behavior and where we were seen.

So yes, the familiarity granted some security but the cost was a loss of independence and individuality. In the 1950's, when I grew up, individuality was not something we strived for. If you think about it, in these tiny apartments, there was literally and structurally no room for the independent thinker.

We grew up among many stories and myths. My mother wanted to be a nurse, but of course, as the oldest of six, she had to go to work. Her father died when she was quite young. Her next two siblings wanted to marry. However, the tradition, at the time, was that siblings be married in chronological order. So my aunt and uncle went and introduced my mother to my father.

My parents were married on September 3rd, 1939. Her next sibling, my uncle, was married December 3rd, 1939 and the next was married March 3rd, 1940. I'm blessed to be able to say my parents, not without their many challenges, had a wonderful marriage.

Life growing up in The Village extended far beyond our apartment walls. Beyond sharing the streets and buildings, we shared a culture. Not just defined, as in my life, by a Southern Italian mother and a Northern Italian father. I might as well have been interracial!

We shared this neighborhood with many musicians and artists who came to claim the Village alongside us. They could afford so little, and we shared our culture with them. It made all of us much richer.

As a family therapist, I learned and practiced and have helped couples and families with "alternative lifestyles." We grew up with "alternative lifestyles." The Bohemian community, the Gay community, the political activists. We lived together. We got to know each other as neighbors. We shared.

My parents business was a dry cleaner, New Supreme Cleaners at 81 MacDougal Street between Bleecker and Houston Streets. Because of an exorbitant rent increase in 1984, my parents could not afford to renew their lease. The now famous, Café Dante, took over the spot by expanding from 79 MacDougal into 81 MacDougal. Many, who became popular and famous, like Bob Dylan and his wife and children, Mary Travers of Peter, Paul & Mary, Patti Smith, Leslie Nielsen, Holland Taylor and many more were my parents neighbors, friends and customers. My parents lent them clothes and outfits off the rack for their auditions with promises that they would be returned. And they were. And sometimes money was lent so their kids could pay for the cab they were taking home from school. Then there were the famous families that lived on MacDougal Street, like the Caruso family and the Colt family, who resided directly across the street in the historic, landmark, MacDougal-Sullivan Gardens.

As a fellow shopkeeper and business owner, my parents witnessed the openings of such famous places as the Café Wha? Gaslight Café, Village Gate and the infamous Comedy Club on MacDougal Street. They enjoyed, of course, Washington Square Park and its chess players and the resilient Café Reggio.

Recognizing this legacy, we have the opportunity to understand the privilege we have when we say, "I grew up in "The Village," Greenwich Village!

RICARDO PECORA

Does Anybody Speak Spanish?

I was born November 4th, 1946, in Greenwich Village on the lower West side of Manhattan. The Village was a magnet for the different, the odd, and weirdoes. Artists, sculptors, intellectuals, writers, poets, musicians, gays, socialists, communists, mixed race couples and junkies all assembled there and called it home. Why this area was ripe for free thinkers, freedom lovers, the counter-culture and people that needed to express themselves, I have no clue.

Every spring and fall the Village turned into an outdoor Arts Gallery. Visitors and locals walked the streets enjoying or criticizing what they saw. The "Beat Generation" began and ran its course. Half a century later some still use words like "cool" and "groovy."

The music scene of the 50's and 60's in the Village started with the rebirth of Folk Music and encompassed Jazz, Blues and Rock & Roll. Music venues like the Bitter End, Café au Go-Go, Gerde's Folk City, the Village Vanguard and the Blue Note were thriving.

Singers and songwriters including Bob Dylan, Pete Seeger, Peter, Paul & Mary started out in coffee houses sometimes located in the basement of tenement buildings. Artists like Andy Warhol and writer/poets like Alan Ginsberg lived in the Village. My friend Bob Daly lived in an apartment above a coffee house featuring Van Morrison. I can just imagine what it was like listening to him sing "Into the Mystic" live, so soon after he wrote it.

I will never forget seeing Nina Simone at a standing room only performance at the Village Vanguard. From my vantage point, I could only see her head above the piano. Her brilliant turquoise eye shadow blazed in her spotlight as she sang the best version of Dylan's "I Shall Be Released" I ever heard.

Washington Square Park was a central location in the Village scene, located across the street from the New York University Campus. The focal point of the park was a huge replica of the "Arc d'Triompe" which dominates the beginning of 5th Avenue. At the base of the Arc was a large open area where musicians, poets, political proselytizers, adherents of religious fire and brimstone and druggies of all appetites congregated to express themselves or to entertain the crowd, which consisted of locals, and tourists, alike. In the summer, during the week, the large circular fountain would sprout water to assist parents in keeping their children cool and occupied.

Often, during the weekend, in the evening, when the large crowds were hoping for some entertainment, a huge strong Black man who called himself "King Brown," would sit atop a makeshift throne in the park. It was a heavy wooden office chair that he carried around with him. He would sit in it, with a crown on his head, and dispense inflammatory rhetoric. Often, he would challenge onlookers to fistfights! He was obliged by an enforcer for the local Mafioso. The younger challenger was very big, better muscled and more handsome than King Brown.

What a sight to watch these brutes take turns punching each other in the face (Thank you very much, now it is my turn.) Thunderous swings from huge fists would continue until both sides were worn out. They would shake hands and discuss when to meet again. The adrenalin was palpable and the crowds ate it up.

In another part of Greenwich Village, a large Billboard over 7th Avenue and Christopher Street declared in bold letters: "Man's Country." It signaled the beginning of a large gay community extending from the sign to the docks on the Hudson River waterfront. A few hundred feet from the sign the police raided the Stonewall Inn on Christopher Street just off of Sheridan Square. This time, late night of June 27th and early morning of June 28th, 1969, the gay community rioted and fought back. This event is generally believed to be the single most important catalyst leading to the LGBTQ liberation movement.

While all this was occurring in the Village, the backbone in the area was four Catholic Church parishes. Our Lady of Pompeii, St. Anthony of Padua, St. Joseph's and St. Veronica's. The parishioners of the first two institutions were mainly Italian and the last two Irish in ethnicity. These churches were formed when immigrants moved into this area of low rents. Lower middle class, hardworking, God fearing people who voted Democratic and whose children were educated and became either teachers or civil servants.

My parents were born in Italy and I am first generation American. We lived across the street from Our Lady of Pompeii Church and elementary school, at the convergence of Carmine Street, 6th Avenue and Bleecker Street. There is a triangle there called Father Demo Square which is a small park dedicated to an early priest and pastor of the parish.

The building we lived in was a 5 story tenement. Each floor had three apartments and three single toilets in the hallway. There were no showers or tubs in the original apartments. Over the years, some tenants retrofitted upgrades to include showers in the kitchen. We did not. I was five years old when the owner/landlord brought heat and radiators into the building, most likely, by law. The pipes were visible in the corners of rooms and covered with asbestos so people wouldn't get burned. No one knew the dangers then, of using such materials. Also, the age of the building was a mystery? However, Edgar Allan Poe was purported to have stayed at 13 Carmine Street.

Growing up, the church played a big part in our lives. The Catholic Church's teachings were more Old Testament than Jesus' love and forgiveness philosophy. It was more like an eye for an eye and a tooth for a tooth. The nuns wore black and white habits, no nuances. The pastor, Father Albanese, occasionally taught Catechism classes but was rarely see, except at mass. He was a larger than life figure and what he preached was gospel!

Father Albanese did enjoy supervising the singing at our 8th grade graduation ceremony. He heard my singing at practice and in front of everyone told me at graduation I was to move my lips but there had better be no sound emanating from my mouth.

I was an altar boy, and for some reason, I was given the special honor of serving at the 7 am mass on Saturday for an entire year. (Now, I think I know why I was given that honor, because everyone else turned it down.) Not only did my mother say I would do it, she stayed up all Friday night to make sure I made it to church on time, the following morning. Father Ricci, always served the 7 am mass on Saturday. He couldn't speak English so if any of us did something heinous or embarrassing, we would go to him for confession. He had no idea what we attested to but he knew why we chose him, so he provided extra penance accordingly. He was a short stubby man about 70 years old. It didn't take long to figure out why he was assigned the early mass on Saturday.

When the altar boy was pouring water and wine from the cruet over his fingers in his gold chalice, he would allow only a few drops of water before making an upward movement to cut off the flow. When I poured the wine into the chalice, it was more like counting up to thirty before he stopped me, or before the cruet ran dry. Father Ricci had a drinking problem, and a W.C. Fields ulcerated nose, to prove it.

As teenagers, we would meet at dusk, after dinner, on the weekends, to walk around the Village looking for some excitement. The possibility of getting into some mischief was always present. We wanted to drink alcohol but were too young to purchase it. One of us had a brilliant idea: find a homeless man, or in that era, a drunk vagrant, give him $10 to buy vodka or scotch and let him keep the couple of dollars change. It usually worked like a charm until one sot thought he could make a run for it, keeping the booze and the tip. These men were so feeble, we could walk faster than they could run. From then on, we stationed ourselves to cover all avenues of escape.

One Friday night, after our customary routine did not result in any thrills, the four of us: Richie Palandrani, Al (Butch) Canecchia, Dennis Genovese and myself, were heading home. We were walking down MacDougal Street, which was as busy as a New Orleans street at *Mardi Gras*. We turned left onto Minetta Lane. This short cut to our family apartments is poorly lit, but familiar to us, as we often took it. We were all clowning around due to our earlier consumption of spirits. We noticed a commotion ahead of us, half-way down the block. There was a crowd gathered and a police car with its lights flashing. Like a moth to a flame we were drawn to the energy and excitement in the air.

When we reached the throng, we noticed two young men with their backs to the wall, with two policemen, about ten feet away, questioning them. The crowd consisted of about 12-15 people. The young men spoke no English and the cops no Spanish, making communication difficult. One of the cops turned to the crowd beseeching, "Does anyone speak Spanish?" After a long pause, Dennis chimes in saying, "Yeah, I speak Spanish." The officer instructs Dennis to ask the two perpetrators what their name is. Dennis turns to the suspects and says, "The El Copo wants to know your El Nameo."

The three of us look at Dennis, then at the cops. Dennis looks at the cops, then us. All four of us hightail it out of there as fast as we can, knowing they wouldn't chase us do their involvement in the ongoing situation. We reached 6th Avenue and continued to run till we reached Father Demo Square. There we sat on a bench, calmed down and eventually made our way home.

Robert Perazzo

Holy Saturday

It was a warm "Holy Saturday" night in 1960. I had to be home before all my friends. As I left Leroy Street Park, on my way home, I passed Guido's Bar on the corner of Leroy and Bedford Streets.

I looked into the bar and saw some of my neighborhood heroes. Richie Guillian, Robert (B-Bomb) Roxbury, his brother Bernie, Jerry Vaughn and Richie (Bambino) Pedrini.

To my amazement, they saw me and invited me in to join them at the bar. Now this was the biggest event that could have happened in my life. However, the opposing fact was that I lived just up the block and either my mother or father could easily see me.

I overcame me apprehension of parental oversight and went in. I was put in a bar seat right next to Jerry Vaughn and handed a small glass of beer. I was at the height on my "coolness" and couldn't wait to share my adventure with my classmates at Ester Sunday mass the next morning.

While sitting at the bar I realized Jerry had gone. I looked outside and noticed Jerry had walked across the street to the other bar on the opposite corner. He had started a fight with two other guys. They were going at it in the middle of the street.

Suddenly, all the guys in both bars piled out onto the street to join in the fracas. In a sheer moment of brain freeze, I became involved in the brawl. Actually, I stood behind B-Bomb and made believe I was kicking the guys from the other bar.

Out of nowhere, two huge Irish Detectives from the 6th Precinct roll up in an unmarked car, with guns drawn.

My whole life flashed before me. At that moment, I was thinking of prison time, as opposed to what my parents would do to me. Facing the worst possible scenario of my brief life, I did what any trapped rat would do. I Lied!

I started to cry and told the cops that my mother had cancer. Luckily, he bought my B.S. story, kicked me in the butt, and sent me on my way. Needless to say, I stayed on the straight and narrow, after that.

Dominick Perruccio

The Summer Of 68

This chapter is dedicated to Michael Asciak, friend and schoolmate who died in the World Trade Center on 9-11-01. Michael was 47 years old.

I also want to shout out to six more friends that I grew up with!

1968 was a glorious time in our lives in the neighborhood. We just graduated from Our Lady of Pompeii (OLP) our grammar school and we were off to see the world, or so we thought. This was a new challenge to us while maturing and freedom was our main priority. Keep in mind, at age 13, most of us weren't even shaving yet, but we thought we knew it all but our actions showed how naïve and immature we actually were.

OLP was located in the heart of the Village where two famous crossroads intersected. Bleecker and Carmine Streets. It also was highly visible to 6th Avenue, (currently named the Avenue of the Americas) with its enormous domed bell tower on top of the church. The church and school complex is an iconic landmark known to many and appreciated for its architecture inside and out. It resembles a cathedral that one might see in Italy. The church was founded in 1892 and the school in 1930.

Sadly, the school closed its doors in 2020, due to low attendance and poor management. It's the sign of the times, many private/religious schools throughout the city are suffering the same fate. So, as sad that I am that this happened, OLP had a good 90 year run of which I occupied 9 of those years, Kindergarten through eighth grade.

School Structure:

Each grade had two separate classes due to size limits. My graduating class had 29 students, 12 girls and 17 boys. After some basic research, I found that 5 boys have passed away, some at a very young age. I'll list them in the order that they passed:

Robert Tedesco
Mark Vieira
Michael Asciak
Anthony Agostino
Jerry Ottomanelli

The next two boys were our friends but were not in the class of 68. Stanley Parodi went to St. Anthony's School and Thomas Murphy went to OLP, a year older than us.

Some general information on these 7:

4 died under the age of 21.
3 died under the age of 60.
4 died of natural causes.
3 died violently (gunshot or terrorism).
6 of the 7 lived within two blocks of the OLP complex
less than 500 feet away.

Here is a synopsis of my grades and teacher comments taken from my report cards. I'm certain my classmates had similar reviews. Then again, there were students who were very intelligent, they studied and applied themselves. The report card had a front and back. Front were numerical grades, rear was basically human development. The three "C" were for conduct, cooperation and courtesy.

Grade 1. Miss Coleman 88 average. All A's on back
Grade 2. Sister Antoinette 79, Mostly B
Grade 3. Miss Carolan   88   Mostly A
Grade 4. Sister Regina   78   Mostly A
Grade 5. Miss Masi   79   Mostly B

Here's where it slides downward:
Grade 6. Sister Vincent   76   Split B and C
Grade 7. Sister Raphael   77   Mostly c and D
Grade 8. Sister Mary Paul – CANNOT LOCATE CARD- I BURNED IT!

I did graduate that year and went on to La Salle Academy H.S. (Christian Brothers.)
RECAP:

> Strongest subject, best grade was Religion
> Weakest was Reading, go figure?
> I always earned a C in the three "C'S".
> My absolute best was Personal Appearance,
> Always an "A" LOL.

Robert Tedesco – lived on Bedford Street

We called him Bobby T. He was named after his father who was also called Bobby T. So it was junior and senior. From about the 6th grade on most of our friends hung out in Carmine Street Park. Now, since the park had another entrance on Downing Street, some would argue that it was named Downing Street Park. Although having graduated with Bobby, he was closer in friendship to Stanley and Marky primarily because they lived closer to each other. I lived about 6 blocks away so I was closer to Michael and Jerry. Also, I went on to H.S. with them. After grammar school, friendships scatter and more so after H.S. And of course, interest in the opposite sex can derail friendships simply because there are only a certain amount of hours in a day. We basically formed smaller sub groups. Bobby seemed to wander off the reservation to a new group of friends from the Prince Street area of the Village. I knew the group, stayed with them a while, then moved on. Bobby was in uncharted and unsafe waters with this group, and was pretty much on his own, with no one to watch his back. One day he had an argument with one of the guys. The guy shot him in the head, killing him. The police arrested him and he went to prison.

It was a very sad time in the neighborhood. Bobby's murder decimated his entire family. They never recovered from it. Booby T was only 16 years old.

MARK VIEIRA – lived on Carmine Street.

We called him Marky. He had an older brother named Pauly. Pauly's friends were older than us and were notorious ball breakers that would bully us. That's how it went years ago. We in turn, would bully the group below us. It was a trickle- down effect. However, we were not as vicious. One might argue that point.

Marky was a tough kid, physically strong. That didn't matter to us pranksters. One day Anthony Agostino (Auggie) and I, hatched up a plan to gather up some dog feces, wait till he was in the tub, and drop it on him through his skylight. Marky lived on the top floor. We figured out his schedule, went up to his roof and BOMBS AWAY! He was pissed, we ran for our lives. He wanted to kill us. We ran to our friend Tweet, who had an older brother, Jo-Jo, who calmed Marky down.

Another vicious incident occurred one night while drinking and walking the neighborhood. Jo-Jo decided he wants to test his punching power on Marky's jaw. Marky had this big, bulbous round head. A massive target. We were in the warehouse district on Van Dam Street. Jo-Jo zeros in on that big melon and wales him a shot on the jaw. Marky gets rocked. He is wobbly and falls hitting his head on a corrugated metal accordion garage door. He didn't get knocked out, he was too drunk. When he recovered a few seconds later the first words out of his mouth were "Why Is my head so big?"

Marky also drifted out of the neighborhood as he got older. We were all headed in a bad direction. Once alcohol entered our lives, it was a progressive downward slide. Marky enlisted in the Air Force. We would sometimes see him when he came home on leave. The military did not settle his life. He contracted hepatitis in Thailand destroying his liver and killing him at the age of twenty.

STANLEY PARODI –lived on Bedford near Houston.

Stanley lived about two buildings away from Bobby T. He grouped up with Bobby and Marky so we called them the Three Musketeers. He was our age but went to St. Anthony's School. His building was of equal distance between OLP and St. Anthony, so his parents made that choice. He's our only friend that hung out with us that did not attend OLP. His father was a low level loan shark called Vinny Moustache, an associate in the Genovese Family. His parents were older than ours, Stanley was their youngest child. He didn't play many sports and always seemed frail. Most of us were skinny, always on the Go-Go-Go. Obesity was uncommon back then. We were always moving like sharks. We only went home to sleep. Stanley died very young of natural causes. I think it was a brain aneurysm. He was in his teens.

THOMAS MURPHY – lived on Carmine next to Polichetti Bakery.

We named him "Murph the Surf", the name was stolen from the famous real life jewel thief/cat burglar. Tommy was one cool cat! His cousin Charlie De Bellis was my lifelong friend and was a neighborhood icon and power house. We go back 60 years, starting our friendship at 6.

So back to Murph. Growing up with him in our group we could see that he was always fast tracking. At age 15, he was the first to be professionally tattooed. I, on the other hand, bought a ten dollar tattoo kit from the back of a magazine ad and decided to develop my artistry skills at the expense of my friends, who would volunteer to be scarred for life.

In the beginning, I kept it basic, with dots in the shape of a cross on their wrists. Me, my brother Cooker, Charlie and Auggie all fell victim to this ink experiment. No big deal. If you wanted to hide it, the wrist could be covered with a leather band, which was popular in the late 60's with the so called Hippie movement. More importantly, our parents would not detect it. I soon retired after my botched attempt at Ink Art. Thank God for that decision.

Murph was another guy who didn't fit in. He wandered off the reservation also, despite being Charlie's cousin. As time went on, everyone would ask, 'where's Murph?" No one had a clue. Then the rumors followed. He was hanging with a rough crowd in the Times Square area which was a cesspool back then. Pimps, hustlers, junkies, pornography, the whole nine yards. The Devil's Workshop! We called the area "forty deuce." It was bad ass and extremely dangerous. Murph developed a drug habit and much, much more. A parents' worst nightmare!

Tommy Murphy, AKA Murph, The Surf made the front pages of all the N.Y. newspapers one morning when he died in a hail of bullets with the NYPD. He shot it out with them and wasn't going to be taken in alive. My opinion was that it was suicide by cop, and if so, he invented it. I think he was disgusted with his lifestyle, having grown up in a normal middle class Catholic home. He had a good family structure. Somewhere along the line he drifted and started going deep and dark. No one could control him. He was a Type A, all the way, with his personality, which was common to most in my group.

The mean streets of NYC ate him up and spit him out. Into the gutter where he died. He was very young, I believe he was in his late teens. Another sad day and wasted potential in life.

MICHAEL ASCIAK – lived on Bedford close to Carmine.

We called him "the count" because he had facial hair at a young age which included sideburns in high school. His ancestors were from Malta, so sometimes I called him "the Maltese Falcon." He probably started shaving in the 6th grade. I went to school with him from Kindergarten through high school. We also hung around with each other. He was a bright student who applied himself and became an accountant after graduating from college.

In grammar school we would cheat off of him during tests. We were always gaming the system. He was a good kid in spite of the bad influences we were. He had good parents who kept him under a watchful eye. They had established rules in their household. Mike made them proud and abided by their requests. Maybe sometimes bending them a little. Nobody in our group was a Saint!

As we got older, about the age of 15, we had a social club a block and a half from his building. Most of would drink beer and alcohol there. I can't recall Mike drinking. On occasion, we would have him sit on the window bench seat and scream a chant at him in German. This little charade was orchestrated by Vinny Cavaliero, who we called horse, because of his last name. Horse learned German at Xavier H.S. Mike was complacent with this, it amused him to be the center of our attention. This soon earned Mike a new nickname. "THE FUHRER,' which translates from German as LEADER. What a bunch of psychos! The whole neighborhood heard this bizarre chant when we did it. We would leave the door open so they would get the full impact!

BASIC REENACTMENT OF THE CHANT:

Milkey Doran would holler "Achtung" Meaning attention. We would all line up facing The Fuhrer. Then horse would yell, "EINS-ZWEI-DREI" Meaning one-two-three. Then we would holler, "SIEG – HEIL" meaning hail to victory. As we screamed the Sieg-Heil, we would all raise our right arms in Salute! We did this several times, "you can't make this stuff up." It was real.

I'm sure this behavior is abnormal in Kansas but perfectly acceptable in THE BEDFORD CLUB. I am dedicating this section to my buddy Michael. In spite of hanging around with us, he made a success of himself. He was a good husband and father with a great future ahead as an accountant.

On that fateful day, September 11, 2001, Michael and Robert

O'Shea, another H.S. friend, were working together for a brokerage firm on the top floors of THE TOWERS. They were senselessly murdered by Islamic terrorists. They both were 47 years old.

"HUMAN BEINGS ARE THE ONLY SPECIES ON EARTH CAPABLE OF DOING UNIMAGINABLE VIOLENCE TO EACH OTHER!" This is proof positive.

ANTHONY AGOSTINO – lived on 6th Avenue, opposite Father Demo Square.

We all called him Auggie. He had a younger brother named Robert who we called Bobby or Little Auggie, even though he was bigger in size. They had great parents named Dorothy and Tony Sr. who everyone called Tony Black, because of his deep black hair. Both brothers hung out with us, especially as we got older. Two stand-up guys that were not only trustworthy, but were enjoyable to be around. They enjoyed having a good time – wine, women and song, as the saying goes.

One day we hatched a plan to do an "eat and beat" at Emilio's on 6th Avenue across from his house. This was when Emilio's was attached to Gill's Steak House. There were two separate outside entrances spread wide apart and inside there was a wall separating the two. The plan was to eat at Emilio's, go to the bathroom, then exit out from Gill's. The plan worked but it was flawed. We did get away with it, but only temporarily. Everyone in the neighborhood knew each other. Tony Black was well known, for several reasons, one being he was in the restaurant business. He was a *maître d'*. Auggie went home and the next day he had to pay the bill. Another embarrassing moment for our parents.

We also played a lot of sports in the neighborhood. Auggie played limitedly. He mostly enjoyed playing cards and gambling. One year the stars in heaven aligned with our softball team. Auggie played right field for us. It was a rag tag team very loosey/goosey. One of the coaches was named Anthony (Goose). He was a great guy who volunteered his time to the team. Sadly, Goose died young with a heart attack at 40 years old. He was following in the footsteps of his father, who also died young. We played for our school, OLP and won the championship in 1972. We were all proud of this accomplishment, we brought honor to our neighborhood.

Shortly after our championship the season ended. We were all around 18 and driving. Coincidentally, 18 was the drinking age and we added that to our resume.

That made us dangerous pranksters and goof balls. We soon reported to a local high powered gangster named "Johnny the Bug." He was a friend to my family. My mom and uncle worked for him. Now, a bunch of my friends including Auggie formed a group called "THE DIRTY DOZEN." We began hanging around and socializing with him.

We now graduated from "pranksters" to "gangsters." We had our own club, drove fast flashy cars and enjoyed life to the fullest and beyond, with no boundaries. Being mobile, allowed us to explore the 5 boroughs of NY and the areas close by in NJ. We soon lost interest in our club and closed it. Yet, we are still, to this day, recognized by everyone in the neighborhood, as "BEDFORD CLUB," as if it were tattooed in their memory banks. Some went to Johnny the Bug's club, a place to hang their hat and fraternize with him and other mobsters. Johnny's club was close by on King Street and you had to follow Johnny's unwritten rules to hang there.

Auggie kind of drifted away when our club closed. He remained in the neighborhood and we would occasionally run into each other since we had similar interests and lifestyles. This kept him relatively safe from harm. He didn't suffer the fate of Bobby T or Murph the Surf. Unfortunately, he died a few years ago of natural causes. He was about 60 years old.

GEROME OTTOMANELLI – lived on 10th and Bleecker

We called him Jerry or Otto. I lived one block away on Christopher and Bleecker so I was good friends with him from Kindergarten through H.S. Jerry came from a large family with many siblings and the Ottomanelli name is well known in NYC. His relatives owned the famous butcher shop on Bleecker, a restaurant uptown and a sports/gun shop in NJ.

Growing up we went bike riding all over Manhattan. Sometimes we would hop the Staten Island ferry and ride around there. We were always active as youngsters. We would walk down to the Hudson River. It was about 5 blocks away. We called that area the docks, not the river. Lots of mischief and adventure happened there. Childish things: like the unauthorized boarding of barges and boats that were tied to the bulkheads on the river, climbing over fences and walls to gain access to abandoned buildings, warehouses and piers so we could temporarily claim them as our clubhouses until we were chased away. We would smoke cigars and cigarettes there, buying them from vending machines that were located in the seedy merchant marine hotels that years ago dotted the waterfront. It was very adventurous. We felt like Huckleberry Finn on the Mississippi. The sights and smells of the river were intoxicating! We would also light fire crackers, M80's and cherry bombs, throwing them in the water to watch them detonate underwater, blowing a fountain of water into the air above.

We'd fish for eels, catching them and hauling them back to the neighborhood. Then we would release them in Leroy Street Pool. That was our version of "catch and release."

Now here's a physics experiment that I discovered. I lived one block from Jerry in a 16 story high rise building. He lived in a multi-cultural tenement of all nationalities, with lots of children. We would go on my roof and throw eggs and water balloons at the kids that lived in Jerry's building. The kids, mostly Puerto Rican, never knew where the barrage was coming from. They did not suspect my building, because they always looked across the street at neighboring structures. Good thing we never got caught. They were tough kids and it would have started a neighborhood rumble!

After high school we kind of separated. I moved to Staten Island and then NJ. Jerry moved to Queens and then Long Island. We did see each other occasionally while working in NY. We both worked on 53rd and Park Avenue. He worked for Citibank in their headquarters.

I worked for Diebold Safe Company at their headquarters. We sometimes went to lunch together, in his cafeteria. After I transferred to NJ, we lost touch with one another. Sadly, Jerry passed away a few years ago of natural causes. He was in his early 60's.

So that concludes THE SUMMER AND GRADUATING CLASS OF 68. MY friends that are no longer with us are truly missed. Some were cheated out of life by dying at an early age. Nobody knows the reason or can give an answer as to why it happens. My opinion – it's all Divine Intervention. It is God's will. Especially in my case, I ask the question, "Why am I still here?" I don't believe in luck or coincidence and I'm not that intelligent.

PERHAPS I'M STILL HERE TO DOCUMENT THE PAST?

THE END!

Francine Raggi

Do Black People Cry Black Tears Do Bad Things Happen To Good People?

    Ah! Yes, we grew up in Greenwich Village in a corner building that faced both Bleecker and Sullivan Streets, with 3 apartments on each floor of a five story walkup. We were on the first floor right next to the superintendent of our building. Al Taylor and his wife Louise and her father. If mom needed an egg, I had two choices, walk out the front door of the apartment, go a few steps and knock on Mr. and Mrs. Taylor's door, or climb out our living room window onto the fire escape. There I could check out what was happening on Sullivan Street as I knocked on the window of the Taylor family to ask for an egg. Well, yes, you can guess my choice.
    Al, Mr. Taylor, appeared to a little eight year old girl, in retrospect, the size of Michael Clarke Duncan, the black actor who won an Oscar for his role in the 1999 blockbuster, The Green Mile. He towered over me and was twice the girth of my brother Dennis, who was, at 15 years old, close to six feet tall and skinny. Al and Dennis bonded so easily over their love of fishing. Fishing, Greenwich Village … huh? On many a day, Dennis would wake up and skulk about in two of the four rooms of our apartment, getting ready to meet Al at 4:45 am, to go fishing. A boat they could catch, a pier, wherever, they lugged their rods, reels and metal boxes filled with myriads of

lures and home- made sinkers. Oh! I divert for a moment. Do you remember when your grandmas would melt the lead sinkers on a special Saint's feast day and pour the melted lead very slowly into ice water to decipher what forms determined for the future of the one that melted the lead was poured for? Another vivid memory of mine.

Hmmm? Did Al and Dennis catch anything? I do recall eels, nerves jumping, frying in grandma's black frying pan, having been caught out of the Hudson River. And, as I remember, no one in the Village questioned what a 15 year old, tall, lanky young man, was doing with this big, black man at 5 am in the morning, lumbering on the streets of Greenwich Village.

We were blessed to be raised in a community where different races, creeds, lifestyles traversed the streets with little opposition, unless of course, they were there looking for trouble. How wonderful to meet people from all over the world while growing up there, yet, feel safe walking the streets at 11 pm to get the Daily Mirror or the News for my dad each evening, when I was 11 or so.

And it wasn't only Dennis who lumbered along with Al. Many others followed in Dennis' footsteps, long after that tragic, horrid, still deeply existing in my being, that day, and thereafter: November 4, 1955. On that day, Dennis at 15 years of age, was shot and killed at the home of his friend Richard, who just turned 16, by a 22 caliber rifle that was awarded to Richard for good marksmanship from the *Tiro a Segno Club,* still located on MacDougal Street. Richard, only 15 years old at the time when he received the rifle, was underage to receive a firearm. Since the *Tiro a Segno* catered to Police Captains, Fire Chiefs, politicians, Judges and the like, the case was pushed under the rug. Why was Richard filing down the trigger? Why did Richard have a bullet in the chamber? Why did Richard's shooting finger find its way to the trigger? Richard was never held accountable for the crime, for if he was found guilty, the cub would have been culpable for providing the rifle to an underage recipient. Dennis died at St. Vincent's Hospital, with Father Louis Gigante giving him the Last Rites. Father Gigante told my parents Dennis asked, "Will I go to heaven Father?" just before expiring.

When my mother and father came home from the hospital, walking slowly up the staircase to our first floor apartment, I naively ran out to give Dennis some candy my aunt had brought to our home that evening. I asked, "Where is Dennis?" My mother, in anguish, screamed out several times, "Dennis is dead!" What is death to an eight year old? Mr. and Mrs. Taylor, Al and Louise, hearing my mother's laments stepped out onto the landing. When they realized what my mother was screaming ...Yes, black people do cry black tears and lots of them! Yes, bad things happen to good people!

The Greenwich Village community was shocked and offered much comfort to the family. Understandably, the family was never the same. However, on January 6, 1957, the Epiphany, God's Gift, we were blessed with a premature beautiful little boy, who after spending almost a month in the hospital, came home to us. Michael Louis, as he was named, brought a future and love to our heartbroken family.

This story is not a figment of a child's imagination. The *Tiro a Segno* is still there on MacDougal Street. I do not know if Richard is still in this world. I would hope the club ceased awarding a rifle for good marksmanship after 1955, especially to anyone underage! But who knows? They are still in existence.

Antonia Rosa

Being Married To Tony Orlando

My name is Toni Rosa Noferi. I was not born in Greenwich Village but I have lived there for the past thirty years. I am married to the Tony Orlando look alike, David Noferi. Back in the day, we would go to lots of gigs whether Fab Four or others were performing. Mostly, it was the Folk singer Richie Havens.

Well, one night David and I were at B. B. King's to see Richie perform. As usual, Richie was awesome. I loved when he did the song "Freedom." Of course, we had front row seats, and Richie would mention our names, from time to time. He was always smiling and was a great friend. David and I really miss him. May he Rest in Peace.

On one occasion I had to use the bathroom which was upstairs. David always insisted on following me even though I can pack a good punch. We get upstairs and I use the bathroom, which was very quickly done. When I exit the lavatory, David has two tall, buxom blondes hanging all over him. They were saying, "Oh Tony Orlando, we love you." Well I usually always played along but this one wasn't going to fly.

So I said, "David, who are these two bimbos hanging all over you?" The girls replied, "David, no, it's Tony Orlando. Who are you?" I replied, "I'm his wife, and I'm not Dawn either!"

I told David to take out his I.D. When the girls saw his

identification and the name on it was David Noferi, they smacked their lips saying, "What a fraud." I said, "No he isn't. He did not say he was Tony Orlando. The two of you just assumed so."

Well, as the saying goes, don't assume because it makes an ass out of you, and me, and I am definitely not an ass. I am a five foot two, Sicilian fire eating dragon!

We then went back downstairs to continue watching Richie play and sing. No, I did not give David too much flack. I had gotten used to people thinking he was Tony Orlando. There was quite a resemblance and that carried even greater weight when we were with Richie Havens. Like being married to the mob, I was married to Tony Orlando! (See picture in Photo Gallery of Richie Havens and David Noferi.) You can make up your own mind about the resemblance.

• • • • • • • • ●○○○○○○○ ○ ○

Ralph Sabatino

A Unique Place

Greenwich Village in the late 1950's, and the early 1960's was a unique place. I should know. I was born and raised there.

The coffee houses, social clubs, cabarets, inimitable off-market restaurants, the bohemian lifestyle and a dynamic Italian American community all combined to create a unique atmosphere. Either, as children or young adults, we came to revel living in the Village, at this most unusual and creative time in the chronicles of NYC and the country.

I remember a friend of mine mentioning the actor and social satirist of the time, Mort Sahl, after a visit to a late night show at the Bitter End Café, and a stroll through those back streets of the West Village, unique unto themselves, remarking: "This place is like a closet in a house hidden in the woods. First, you have to find the house in the woods, then the closet. It's buried in time, living by its own set of rules." And, so it was.

On one of those back streets, seemingly forgotten in time, on a Cornelia Street stoop, as a young man in the 1960's, sitting with two of my friends, listening to the radio and trying to figure out what to do next, we hit upon the idea of trying to sing harmony. I'm still not sure how it all began but nonetheless, there we were, three guys started to sing, as if for no other reason, than it was something different to do.

There were three of us; Dennis Genovese, Sergio Bosi and me, Ralph Sabatino. On numerous occasions, Sergio would suggest going to his apartment to listen to his classic collection of Doo-Wop recordings. This was the music of the time for young teenagers. American popular standard music, which was still regarded as the standard of good music in the country, was losing sway to the energy and enthusiasm of Doo-Wop and Rock & Roll. The music of Chuck Berry, The Drifters, The Platters, Dion & the Belmonts, The Del-Vikings and so many, many more, were hypnotic and transformative to teenagers who simply wanted to sing and be part of it all. Listening to old Doo-Wop records was the tonic that inspired us. This was the music of the time we lived in.

Still young, and learning about the business of "making harmony," with a sound that was all the rage, was part of the excitement. Without a barometer to measure, we sounded pretty good, or so we were told, and our journey in the music world had begun. As with all journeys, it starts with first steps, then off we went.

We were, for all intents and purposes, children of the streets. Products of that place called Greenwich Village, yet our sound emanated with a boyish call, espousing hopeful ambition that drew the attention and recognition within the inner circles of the cafes and clubs along Bleecker and McDougal Streets

As time passed, we added more singers to the group. Anthony Madison became our lead singer. This was significant because it made our introduction into the business of the Doo-Wop sound "legitimate," and our look and sound were more a part of the sense and the feel of the time. The hallways of those backstreet apartment buildings became our studios, our home and inner sanctum.

It became a thing to find the hallway or alleyway with the best acoustics. This would include subway stations; where on any given night one could hear the harmonic blending of sounds filtering up through darkened subway platforms, or back alleyways and hallways of old buildings with clothes lines and garbage cans, displaying the rudiments of tenement life adorned all around us.

We would search, as if on a celestial mission, for places with the best echo. Moving from place to place, hallway to subway, to back stairwell to find that elusive sweet echo spot that made all the difference in the world. Sometimes we would garner a small audience or hangers on to listen to the sounds of the street, of Doo-Wop, and the sound of the times. The sweet sound of pure harmony, known as *a cappella*, was electric and engaging.

More singers found their way to our harbor: Daniel Marsicovetere, Al Canecchia and Gerard Madison (Anthony's older brother.) We called ourselves Danny & the Sinceres. Now, with a name, it extended and gave the further impression of stature, and formal acceptance in the world of music, from our perspective, and the music business as a whole.

We felt we had arrived! A turning point in all this early development of the group, and to us all as both singers and performers, came when I first met Robert Andriani, Ziggy, as he was known in the neighborhood. He was a self-taught, gifted singer and musician. A very talented musician. He taught us the art of vocal harmony. It was a great step forward. He was as good a mentor as we could have had in this time of change and growth. We were teenagers, young men finding our way in a world that was changing as fast as the sound of the beat of this new music. This development in our music, this sound we helped endorse and promote, had defined our early lives as young men.

But as time went on, as in life, with many things of that life happening all at once, we would separate as a group and as familial friends; going our independent ways with other singing groups.

As those backstreets of the Village began to cultivate different and new sounds, the changing cultural environment of the early to mid- sixties: the rage, a dead president, Vietnam and social discourse and upheaval – the end of an era was upon us. It happened so fast, we all found our way in separate journeys that took us beyond those hallowed halls and back alleys of the West Village to places we could not have imagined at the time.

Given all this, I have found that memories, in that window of time, brought a sweet reminder of a place that we called home.

I will always remember with fond thoughts the song sung by Daniel Marsicovetere, "Memories Linger On." It has brought back a reminder and recollection of our musical journey through those backstreets, hallways, alleyways and subways. Remembrances of a place and time long gone.

As I have returned to the Village, from time to time, and have thought that if I listened hard enough, I could imagine hearing young men singing sweet harmonies, echoes of a time, sounds of a past caught forever in time, in that closet in a house hidden in the woods.

• • • • • • • ● ○○○○○○ ○ ○

Mitzi Schuster

Happy Days

Growing up in Greenwich Village during the 1950's and 1960's was a time that I will always treasure. At that time, we had no idea how fortunate we were to have the unconditional support of our family and friends.

Grammar school was a challenge at St. Anthony's and Pompeii due to the nuns who resorted to various methods of punishment. At St. Anthony's, Father Arthur was called in to discipline the boys who were multiple offenders. Our pastor, Father Arthur, was very involved in our basketball team, Saturday night dances along with the yearly feast of St. Anthony. This occurred during the first week in June and lasted for ten days. It concluded, with a procession through the neighborhood on June 13, the feast day of St. Anthony. Our neighborhood was a safe place because the local wise guys would not have it any other way.

By the time we got to High School, we ventured out to the other boroughs of the city. Coney Island was a train ride away as Staten Island was a beautiful ferry ride. Ice skating in Central Park in Manhattan was another activity on Saturday during the winter months.

Having a driver's license expanded our activities. One Saturday, we all drove up to Bear Mountain to a ski lodge, called Silver Mine. This was the first time on skis for us all. We took the lift to the top of the mountain and managed to survive the run without any injuries. What we didn't know, was how high this mountain was, because of the fog. When we returned, the next time, on a clear day, we were shocked to see the height of the ski slope.

Listening to music on our small transistor radios was popular. We had such great music growing up. Dances at St. Anthony's and Pompeii, on the weekends, was another great time to get together and have fun.

Looking back, life was simple. We were fierce, brave and so full of hope. That journey continued as some decided to make Greenwich Village their forever home. Others, moved to the suburbs to make home ownership a reality.

Although we moved out of the neighborhood, those lifelong friends will always be with us.

Roger Segalini

Growing Up In The Village In The 1950'S

My name is Roger Segalini. The following is a little preview of what it was like growing up in Greenwich Village in the 1950's.

The West Village mainly consisted of the Irish and Italians. You had your middle to lower class families, (economically) and some groups which defy definition. I'd say, our group, fit the lower middle class – although none of us were aware of it. Vacations were rare, TV was in its infancy, and air conditioning was a luxury. Looking back, I guess, you will never miss what you never had.

We didn't have video games; we had the streets!

Everyone would chip in for a Spaulding ball and play a million and one games, like: stoop ball, stick ball, box ball, hand ball etc. We had the best time for hours. In the winter, it was street hockey with roller skates. In the summer, it was scooters that we crafted ourselves out of a 2X4 piece of lumber and a pair of roller skates split in half, and attached to an orange crate. Most of us attended Catholic school. Our Lady of Pompeii on Bleecker Street, located in the heart of the Village. Recently, they have closed down the school, which leaves a gaping hole in my heart.

The Village was a very safe area. In the summer, you were able to leave your front door open to let a breeze through the apartment without any fear. (Not applicable nowadays.) It was a different world then. We didn't have much, but we were grateful for what we did have. Looking back, it was the best of memories.

One thing we were always taught by our parents, nuns at school, relatives, neighbors, were to be respected. Here's a good example: If I saw one of my neighbors in the street and didn't say "hello," that neighbor would ask my parents, "Why didn't Roger say hello?" My parents would enforce this civility and want an explanation from me. I believe the world is the way it is because not many are taught to respect one another. If you have the opportunity to visit the Village, you won't be sorry.

There, you will find, some of the best restaurants in NYC. I, unfortunately, do not live there anymore. I often visit to relive some of my best childhood memories and see my old stomping grounds. And of course, to purchase specialty Italian items I love. I do keep in touch with some friends from grammar school – one of them being my friend since the 1st grade, Alfred Canecchia. A good friend of mine for over 70 years, who is the editor of this book. Thank you for including me in your project.

Salvatore Tofano

John's Pizzeria – Two Jouneys From Different Directions

The song always came back to me "a long, long time ago, I can still remember, how the music used to make me smile." It was at John's Pizzeria where I first heard it on that old jukebox filled with Doo-Wop and Four Seasons songs. Don McLean's "American Pie."

A few months ago, I needed to get back to the Village. After almost two years locked down or locked up, I needed a pizza fix. Real pizza. The subway ride down to West 4th Street station was long and tedious creating a feeling of built-up anticipation. Once at my destination, it all came back. Bleecker Street was still vibrant after all these years. I passed by Our Lady of Pompeii church on Carmine. Still standing tall overlooking Father Demo Square at the intersection of Bleecker and Carmine Streets. With its Romanesque Revival design and bell tower which chimed magnificently below the blue skies and heavens above. A quick prayer and candle was in order. One "Our Father" and touching Mom and dad's name engraved on the inside door with hundreds of other long forgotten parishioners and families. I stared up at the mural on the circular ceiling and reminisced of days gone by. That mural depicting scenes of the bible, God, angels, Lucifer and heaven and hell, always scared the life out of me. Now it was tame compared to the insanity of the real world.

That mural still held its mystique with all the horror and beauty intertwined. I could hear the echoes of Mr. Nichols playing the organ and a children's choir singing. But the organ did not play and not a voice was to be heard. You could hear a pin drop. I looked around at all the statues, the Stations of the Cross plaques, the exquisite stained glass, and the cylindrical light fixtures that hung from the cavernous ceilings. As a boy, I walked these aisles throughout my childhood and sung many a hymn. I said a few more prayers for all the good things in my life, my family and my health, and a few prayers for those gone. A few dollar bills in the donation box and I genuflected again and gave a final sign of the cross. The wooden doors closed behind me as I made my way toward John's Pizzeria anticipating that it had not changed.

I passed by Our Lady of Pompeii school where many early friendships were formed. I could hear the church bells like it was 1967. Across the street used to be Harry's, where baseball cards, comic books, wax juice candies and button sized candies glued to paper rolls were a special treat, fifty years ago. Mallo Cups, the complete sets of Lost in Space and Batman trading cards and fake wax moustaches and lips that could be consumed. God knows what we were eating! Gumball machines where you could get miniature NFL football helmets or any assortment of rubber monsters for a dime.

Then I passed Leroy Street, where we played during lunch time, under the staring supervision and lock and key of Sister Mary and the nuns. They were undoubtedly influenced by the Gestapo or the guards at Alcatraz. One thing for certain, we were protected, and no one would mess with them. Looking back, some of their methods may be deemed harsh by today's standards, but then again today there is zero discipline. The irony of the pendulum of life that swung as swiftly as the wind. I listened and could not hear the faint sound of familiar voices from the past.

We played dodge ball on the narrow street using the yellowed brick wall of the school and the supermarket as the backstops. One of the younger nuns, our eighth grade teacher, Sister Elizabeth, would referee. She was very hip, nice, and played a mean guitar. She was part of the new era. Young, pretty and forward thinking. In 4th grade, I was pushed playing dodge ball and smashed my head against the yellow brick wall. Miss Curran, my teacher and first school boy crush, had to take me to St. Vincent's Hospital by cab. I got five stitches. I can remember that day when my mother rushed down from her office in the hospital to find me sitting there chomping on a Good N Plenty with crusted blood in my hair. I survived.

Hide and go seek, tag, and trading Topps baseball cards on the stoops of the tenement building next to the school. Sometimes chased away by the landlord. "I'll trade you a Mickey Mantle or a Willie Mays for a Peter Rose and a Carl Yastrzemski." And we played stoop ball and buck- buck also known as Johnny Ride the Pony, much to the chagrin of the nuns. No roughhousing on their watch. Sister Antoinette, the second-grade teacher, sat on a wooden stool selling candy from a big metal box that hung from a strap around her neck. Like a carnival barker "Reese's, Snickers, Clark Bars, Sugar Daddy – 10 cents. Mary Jane, Licorice and candy buttons.' Granny glasses and a tempered Midwest drawl, she was definitely not from New York City. She was about 6 feet tall, walked with a slight limp and spit when she became angry or you raised her ire. With the slightest sign of disobedience, she would become irate and threaten our existence with a face full of saliva spray. "I told you to sssh," she would bark. Sometimes it was a slap or a hair pull. I shudder to think of her dressed in clothes other than a nun's habit.

My thoughts quickly shifted. Across the street was where the original House of Oldies that sold 45's and LP's was. Dion, Beach Boys, Motown, Beatles, Simon & Garfunkel, the Rascals and American Pie. I could still hear those songs embedded in vinyl grooves playing on an old phonograph. And the A & P supermarket long gone replaced several times over and over again. Later on it became a restaurant owned by Al Lewis, who was Grandpa on the Munster's. Al did not know good Italian cooking. Too salty and the pasta was undercooked. *Al Dente*, did not mean rinse for five seconds under hot water.

I was famished as I continued my stroll through time. No more fish stores where the wooden barrels filled with clams or blue crabs were always a draw for curious eyes, hands and bitten fingers. One time, John Tosi and I, stuck our hands in the barrel. He escaped the claws of death, but me? Ouch, as the crab pierced the thumb of my right hand. John Tosi stood there pointing and laughing, until his mother, who was waiting outside Jo Allen's with his kid brother, saw our shenanigans and grabbed him by the ear, dragging him home.

Murray's Cheese store, one of the last remnants of a bygone era, originally on Cornelia, now on Bleecker, where it transformed from a small hole in the wall, to a posh, high-end grocery where hipsters frequented. A few doors down, one of the last bastions of the old guard, the kings of sausage, Faicco's. Family run since the beginning of time. The sawdust on the floor, the sweet and pungent smell of sausage, mixed with the aroma of pickles and cheese. Cans of imported tomatoes stacked side by side with authentic olive oil. It was all coming back. Age and time never eradicated my memory. Across the street, I could still smell the bread baking in Zito's bakery. Closed after 80 years. Squeezed out by greedy landlords. The heat from those ovens in the cellar would make its way up from the bowels below and warm many a passerby on a cold wintry day. Above the store, my great grandmother's window, where she watched from the sill, with a maternal eye over the neighborhood and all her children. Rosario "Nonna" Gambino was a real hero. She lived through it all and would die for her family. Never complained, just soldiered on. Another story for another day.

Downstairs to the left where the cranky Frank Gambino wore a permanent scowl but made the best egg creams around. He sold penny candy to noisy school children and mom's wheeling baby carriages. They are all gone. Fragments of love, hate, fear and honor that once blanketed the neighborhood. Down toward the guitar store where Dylan and Hendrix frequented, and Jimmy (Gambino) the boxer, once caught a man trying to pull off a robbery. Jimmy was a fixture for a while. He lost a title fight then had a few more matches. He was a contender but drug use led to his downfall. He lost his legs and then his pride. He could have been a real prince of Greenwich Village.

My journey was almost complete as my hunger pangs were becoming more intense. A few more memories and steps until I reached my destination. John's Bargain Store where bags of toy soldiers sat on a shelf next to the Brillo pads. The Aphrodisiac run by hippies that sold all kinds of nuts incense and joke novelties like Chinese handcuffs, whoopee cushions and joy buzzers. I once bought the cigarette loads and put one in my father's L & M. He was angry at first, but he loved good jokes and laughed it off. I was lucky.

The pet store on the corner of Morton Street where they had a live tarantula in a cage and piranha in a tank. No one would dare stick their hand in to test the waters. Further down the street was Ottomanelli's butcher. The last hold over of original family owned businesses that remained. Lambs, pigs, rabbits and turkeys hung from hooks in the window with eyes still open. And that famous cardboard poster of three hooded old women with larger than life noses sniffing a piece of Parmesan cheese. Till this day, I really could not tell if they were men or women. I could still hear that delivery bicycle clanging and squeaking that young Joe would ride making local deliveries throughout the neighborhood. And then there was Milton's clothing store for men. It sold shoes, chinos, gloves and woolen hats. Who knows where the time went?

At last I reached my destination. The smell of tomatoes, cheese and baking. As I walked inside the restaurant, the neon sign in the window glowed a bright, amber orange. John's Pizzeria. Port Alba. Wines and Beer. Only recently did I discover that Port Alba referred to an ancient gate in the city of Naples. It was like stepping into a time warp. A cardboard poster read "No Slices." John's Pizzeria, Since 1929.

Inside the restaurant, the strains of the song American Pie, and the ghosts of the past danced through my head. "A long time ago, I can still remember how the music used to make me smile." I sat there in that same wooden booth waiting for two pies fifty years ago. I was twelve. My father asked me "Sal can you run down to John's and pick up two pizzas, one small with anchovies, and one large plain." My father was trusting me with an errand. Manhood was right around the corner. My mother with a half worried look said, "Sal, here is five dollars, be careful. "Can I stop and buy a Manhattan Special too?"

Now, fifty years later, John's once a restaurant filled with familiar faces and families of the neighborhood, was transformed into a destination for young hipsters and single professionals who would act cool and say they ate at John's. Now frequented by tourists and "non-villagers" who "heard it was the best." What do they know? We lived it!

The pizza came piping hot like I remembered. Slightly charred, smoky flavor, crispy cheese and bubbling tomatoes. Baked in the original coal oven at 1000 degrees. Containing only the freshest ingredients. Fresh mozzarella, ripe Italian tomatoes and real olive oil that drenched the charred crust. Burnt lips and blistered tongues were the price you paid for eating too quickly, but somehow, it was worth the price. For the adventurous, your pie could be adorned with anchovies or hot sausage that came from Faicco's a few doors away. The jukebox was long gone. I looked around to assess what had changed and what had not. The faded greenish-brown murals on the walls depicting Italian coastal cities and mountains overlooking the Mediterranean Sea, were still there. Above, the tin ceiling with almost a century of grime and dust, overlooked rusty steam pipes. Framed and signed photographs of forgotten boxers, athletes and once famous celebrities adorned some of the walls. Did those people really eat here?

And then my eyes turned toward the graffiti crusted paneling and it all came back. After almost fifty years. The names and initials of lost lovers faded, covered with a layer of time and grease. Etched in the wood were hearts containing the names Johnny & Marie: Vito was here, for a good time call Debbie – Watkins 9-4067, Mets suck, Yankees are great, Dino blows, JB, BL, MP, Sister Mary, Screw you, Cheesy Jo Jo was here, and Jimmy G. That had to be Jimmy Gambino. And there it was. Barely discernable. Under layers of chicken scratch in the second booth: ST. JT. DM. AG. AP. JD. PP.

My seventh grade boy hood friends. All living their own lives now, except one. Joe Deperrie, who died much too young. He never made it past twenty. The perils of city life took him down. Here were the forgotten fragments of a lost childhood and the mischievous pranks of adolescence.

    I drifted back again. My father said "Sal it's getting late, no procrastinating." At twelve, I made the journey in my high-top black Converse sneakers from Perry and Bleecker Streets. Passing the laundromat, bouncing a Spaulding ball and clutching the five dollar bill in my other hand. Under blue skies, before the skyscrapers would tower over us, I was king. Before the fancy stores would creep into the neighborhood. When we walked to school, fearlessly and slept behind unlocked doors. When milk was delivered to your doorstep in glass bottles. When there was candy for a penny. When stoop ball, stick ball, and skelzie were the games of choice. When church, school and work, were the fabric of our lives. There was Little League, Fathers' Club, Boy Scouts, Police Athletic League, Altar Boys, Knights of Columbus, School dances, egg creams and Midnight Mass on Christmas Eve. The St. Anthony's Feast where it was zeppole's, not fried dough, at 6 for a quarter. When it was safe to walk to school. When you kept your mouth shut. When children should be seen and not heard. When respect your elders was the law of the land. When you had nothing to fear but fear itself.

    Neon signs and neighborhood bars and pizza places abounded. Red telephone booths with rotary phones lined the street corners. Back alleys were always dangerous. It was a time, when your deepest, darkest secrets, were kept that way. A story for another venue.

    I continued toward my destination. A boy becoming a man. Past the grocery stores, past Charles Street where Joey D. lived. Past 10th Street where Phil P. and my friend Anthony once lived. Down past the Fancy Fruits Dairy on Christopher near Sam's bowling alley and Lilac's chocolates. Down past the Pink Tea Cup off Grove and Gristedes, where Tom Checchia was the store manager. He was an old friend of the family. Good man that Tom. And Blaustein's hardware store with barrels of screws and nails laid on the sidewalk.

Ten for a nickel. Past the TV repair shop where Mr. Trombino, dressed in his green uniform, waved hello. Past Lafayette French pastries and an assortment of dry cleaners, restaurants, and various crafts stores that now have faded into the depths of my memory. Past barrow Street where John Tosi lived. We used to shout up at his window, "Hey Tosi, are you coming out to play?"

Across 7th Avenue, where I would run to make it, as the Don't Walk sign flashed. I played that game in my mind, that if you didn't make it across before the sign stopped flashing there would be doom and the earth would implode. Finally, passed Ottomanelli's and arriving at John's Pizzeria. I waited for the pizza my father had ordered. The song came on the jukebox. It was called American Pie. I didn't know what it meant, but it didn't sound like anything I heard before, and boy was it long. Bye Bye Miss American Pie. I waited for the pizza and after eight minutes the song ended. I had a nickel so I played it again. All around people were eating. Mrs. Zuar, the tall waitress with the wire frame glasses was taking orders. I saw a girl from my class with her family. I had a crush on her, Antoinette was her name. She waved as I sat shyly with my crew cut, dungarees and polo shirt. A few more familiar faces sipping Chianti, drinking Sarsaparilla and anxiously awaiting their slightly charred pies. I noticed the brand new paneling that was put up on the walls. Light natural wood. My journey back home was less adventurous. I stopped in Andy's candy store on the corner of 11th Street, for a Manhattan Special, and headed back up the 5 flights of stairs with the still hot pies.

Monday arrived too soon. School was almost out. In 7th grade, we were allowed to go home for lunch. Sometimes we would not go home. Mom would give me a couple of dollars for lunch once every few weeks. I would order sandwiches from Bosco's or the pork store on Carmine. Ham and provolone with hot cherry peppers, cooked salami or roast pork layered on Zito's Italian bread. Sometimes I would eat lunch with each of my grandfathers. Grandpa Cipriano owned a restaurant on Sheridan Square. It was called Salvatore's. He operated it with his wife. I called her Aunt Rose. She was very stern and always wore a blue dress with a brooch. She smelled old, and had a carbuncle on her cheek with hairs protruding from it. I hated getting that wet moustache kiss. I would go there every few weeks and have a veal parmigiana or spaghetti and meatballs, while seated at a table with a red checkered cloth. Tony Bennet, Jerry Vale and Frank Sinatra always were heard in the background. Grandpa C. wasn't nice to many people, but he liked me, since I was his namesake. He was always working and grunted a lot. After lunch, he would open up this large freezer, and give me a tortoni for dessert. On Tuesdays, I would visit my Grandpa Tofano who lived in an elevator building called Breen Towers. He was a gem. A funny man who resembled Walter Matthau. He lived there with his wife, not my real grandmother (she died before I was born.) We called her Aunt Francis. He would always have ham, cheese and tongue. Tongue?! And would hand me a few dollars. SSShh! Don't tell Aunt Francis. His apartment smelled like cigarettes, but he was funny, and I loved him. She was a stern old witch.

One day we all decided to go to John's. We met outside the school entrance at 12:30 pm. Me, John Tosi, Joe Deperrie, Anthony Paolini, Dennis McInerny and Andrew (Cheesy) Genovese. We would make our mark that day. John's Pizzeria for lunch. We sauntered in, greeted Mrs. Zuar, who looked at us skeptically. Trouble was brewing. We ordered two pies and Cheesy started the trend. He pulled out his marker and wrote Cheesy in caps. He was the king of graffiti. He once got caught marking up the subways! No one saw what he did. Then we each took the butter knives and began carving our initials in the virgin wood. Six sets of them. As we covered for each other, all hell broke loose. Mrs. Zuar had a conniption. "What are you boys doing," she yelled! We were in trouble. She had all our phone numbers. When we got home, we all suffered the same fate. My father didn't hit me but I was grounded for a month. I think a few of us may have been smacked around? No spare the rod and spoil the child in this neighborhood. It built character.

The initials grew and grew to widespread proportions and was eventually accepted and encouraged. We started a trend. Fifty years ago, Greenwich Village 1972. It faded away for many, but not for me. I remember. I thought about the family, friends, the church, my great grandmother who sat above in that window. And John's Pizza.

I ate my pizza, savored it and wondered what happened to my buddies? They drifted. Some moved away. They survived. One died. But the music never died. And the church bells will forever ring.

• • • • • • • • • ● ○○○○○○○ ○ ○ ○

Joseph Turchiano

Sweet Sixteen Party
November 29, 1963

My cousin, Lenore Pampalone, moved from Cornelia Street, to Dunkin Hills, Staten Island with her mom and dad (Aunt Judy and Uncle Leo) along with her brother Lenny. To celebrate her sixteenth birthday, a party was planned to include the family along with friends from Staten Island and Greenwich Village, New York.

Unfortunately, the two groups did not mix well and very early that night, on the staircase from the basement, a fight broke out between the Staten Island guys and the Greenwich Village group. This resulted in a broken nose for Eddie Fellini from Staten Island. Legend has it that Gerard Madison was responsible for the damage. He was a highly volatile sort who fought at the drop of a hat. Especially after consuming some alcohol. Word spread quickly on the Island, and before we knew it, there was going to be an even bigger problem. Many cars filled with guys arrived at Lenore's home. The police were called and the group from the Village were escorted to the Staten Island ferry for their safety.

You would think that this was the end of the conflict. However, a few weeks later, on Carmine Street, in front of the Village Pizza, word spread that the Staten Island crew were on their way to retaliate. A call was made from the pizza store to Mickey Japs on Thompson

Street. In no time flat, reinforcements arrived to help. Back in the day, the neighborhood guys would respond as if it were a military operation. Clearly, the Staten Island crew would be outnumbered. Somehow, Staten Island got the message and the conflict was averted.

The neighborhood has changed tremendously and that kind of comradery is a thing of the past. I will always look back at those times with much love and affection for a time gone by, and a place that was a gem.

Paul Volpe

Macdougal Between Bleecker & W. 3rd St.'s

In the 1950's and 1960's, MacDougal Street between Bleecker and West 3rd, was unparalleled. I grew up there and the memories are incredible. There was a blend of beatniks, folk singers, Mafiosos and gays. Their venues were the cafes, clubs and coffee houses.

Starting on the East side of MacDougal from Bleecker, located at 102 MacDougal was Café Espresso, also known as Cheech's Café. I often wondered why the men who frequented the place were always dressed in fine suits. When I matured, I realized it was a Mafia hangout. Also at this address was La Masca, a café and pizzeria. Later, it became El Gaucho, an Argentinian Steak House.

I lived at 104 MacDougal, a tenement from the cold-water flat era. We had two store front businesses on the street level of the building. One was an old fashioned upholstery store, and the other was a fruit and vegetable market that later became Golden Pizza. Under the stairs, the men in suits set up a small desk and chairs to run a gambling operation. 106 MacDougal was home to Frank & Tony's Candy Store. Egg creams, ice cream, malted milks, comic books and sodas were sold there.

114 MacDougal was the site of the Kettle & Fish Bar, where legend proclaims that the poet and musician Bob Dylan, wrote the

lyrics to some of his songs, on napkins they provided. 116 MacDougal had the Gaslight Café, where Bob Dylan, Dave Van Ronk and just about every major folk artist entertained. The corner was occupied by Brickman's Paint Store. It was later replaced by Materas, a Greek diner style restaurant that served excellent apple pie.

On the West side of the street, San Remo's Café and Restaurant, at 93 MacDougal, anchored the corner. On any given day, the Beat Generation, including Alan Ginsberg and Jack Kerouac, along with the locals, drank, together, commiserated with each other and often clashed! At 95 MacDougal, the Rissetto brothers operated a grocery and wine and liquor store.

At 97 MacDougal was Monte's, a Greenwich Village institution. It was a family owned Italian restaurant that is still in operation today, though ownership has changed. 107 MacDougal housed Café Rienzi, a popular beatnik hangout, alleged to be the actor James Dean's favorite. At 109 MacDougal was Scarsi's, a wonderful Salumeria, whose aromas are still with me today. They made the best roast beef sandwiches with grilled onions. The owners pivoted it into the Derby Steak House.

113 MacDougal had the original Minetta's Tavern. A land mark! It is now a high end establishment run by Keith McNally. Across Minetta Lane was Manny Roth's Garage, which became, and to this day still is, the Café Wha? The Swing Lounge at 117 MacDougal, was run by my uncle, and was a well- known Lesbian Bar. It later became the Olive Tree. Caffe Reggio, at 119 MacDougal, is still in operation and is internationally renowned.

Growing up, the amount of kids on this block was huge. Each age group had their own crew. Minetta Lane was our private play area for stick ball, stoop ball and scooter run. The memories will always be with me. Seventy years later, and I feel blessed to have spent time on this block.

Yolanda Volpe

Stuck In A Locker

The year was 1954. I was nine years old and a fourth grader at Our Lady of Pompeii School. It was a warm spring day. One day after school, with my grandmother watching everything from her windowsill, I was roller skating with some friends from the block. Although I considered myself a good skater, I wasn't that day. I was on a slight incline on the sidewalk and lost my balance. I fell directly on my arm and intense pain immediately ensued.

As the pain increased, I started to cry. I went home to my mother and didn't think I had hurt it that bad. She ignored my tears and told me that I needed to do my homework. Since it was my left arm, and I am left handed, it was very difficult to accomplish that task. Through the pain I managed to complete the work. The next day, I woke up and my arm felt even worse. We went to the doctor on 6th Avenue and Bleecker, Dr. Peccorara. He confirmed that my arm was broken and my mother felt terrible. The doctor sent me to St. Vincent's Hospital where my arm was put in a cast.

About a week after that, one of my girlfriends had a crush on a boy, we'll call him John. She and I decided that the two of us would look in his school locker for evidence of any reciprocation of amorous feelings! Because of my broken arm, I hung back, letting her do the bulk of the investigating.

While my friend was looking through John's locker, she heard the nuns coming down the hallway. She ran off and left me behind. I didn't want to run with my cast, so the only thing I could think of doing, was to hide inside John's locker. I squeezed in and closed the door behind me. Not a good idea. I got stuck in there and couldn't get out! I stayed in there for a while. Then the bell rang and I had to get to class. Now I don't know what to do? My girlfriend returned to look for me. She tried to pry me out, but I was really stuck. Unfortunately for me, she had to tell Sister Marie of my predicament.

Sister Marie came and opened the locker, and there I was. I started crying and she was admonishing me and informing me that she would call my mother. After many tries, I was dislodged from the locker. Sister sent me to the Principal's office. I got detention and had to stay after school. I also got punished from my mother. I wasn't allowed out of the house for a week. All this over a boy, who turned out, had no interest in my girlfriend. All this for nothing! However, even if the outcome isn't what you want it to be, you should always help out a friend.

• • • • • • • • ● ○ ○ ○ ○ ○ ○ ○ ○ ○ ∘ ∘

Carol Ann Zuar

Mother Doesn't Always Know What's Best

While this may not be a story of a group of kids hanging on a corner somewhere in the Village, it is about two people who were born and raised there.

Michael Sciarillo and I (Carol Zuar) we're not just friends and next-door neighbors but also indirectly related. Michael's mother Margaret, was my Aunt Beatrice's first cousin. Our doors were side-by-side on the first floor of 272 Bleecker Street. Michael and his family were my family. I looked up to his older sisters and often were given their high-heeled shoes' hand -me-downs to practice how to walk in them. We were all very close.

I am the oldest of three brothers. Needless to say, there were many bats, balls and rifles to play with in our apartment. About the time I was around 16 years old, my brothers were becoming involved in weightlifting. Our apartment had a very long hallway and that's where they would keep the barbells. One day I bragged to Michael that I could press 100 pounds overhead. He didn't believe me and stood there with his arms crossed over his chest like he was waiting to watch me proof it. We loaded the barbells with the 100 pound weight. I bent down and jolted it up so fast, only to catch him in the crotch. He fell to the floor grabbing his private parts and moaning in agony! I screamed to my mom, who was in the kitchen, 'Mom, I hurt Michael with the barbells." She screamed back, "Don't worry, Just rub it honey, Just rub it for him." Michael was crying and laughing at the same time!

• • • • • • • ● ○ ○ ○ ○ ○ ○ ○ ○ ○

CONTRIBUTORS

WITH PUBLISHED WORKS

Peter Arcuri
    Espiritus
    peterarcuri@yahoo.com

Alfred Canecchia
    Greenwich Village Vignettes
    Recollections of a Truant Officer
    New York City: In Small Spaces
    aljocain45@gmail.com
    www.alfredcanecchia.com

Paula De Nicola Chapman
    Penny's Song
    The Supplier
    paulachapmanauthor@gmail.com
    https://irtprods.wixsite.com/paulachapmanauthor

Kathleen Firth
    The Back of the Rooster's Tail
    (available at: Amazon.com)
    hometownvoice@outlook.com

Charles Messina
Stomping Ground: Growing Up in Greenwich Village (with Dominick Perruccio)
The Wanderer (musical play opening in March 2022 at Paper Mill Playhouse with anticipated Broadway debut to follow.)
notoutside@aol.com

Dominick Perruccio
Stomping Ground: Growing Up in Greenwich Village (w. Charles Messina)
Nicholasconst7@yahoo.com

Salvatore Tofano
Stories From the Windowsill (pending, in pre-publication)
stofano@optonline.net